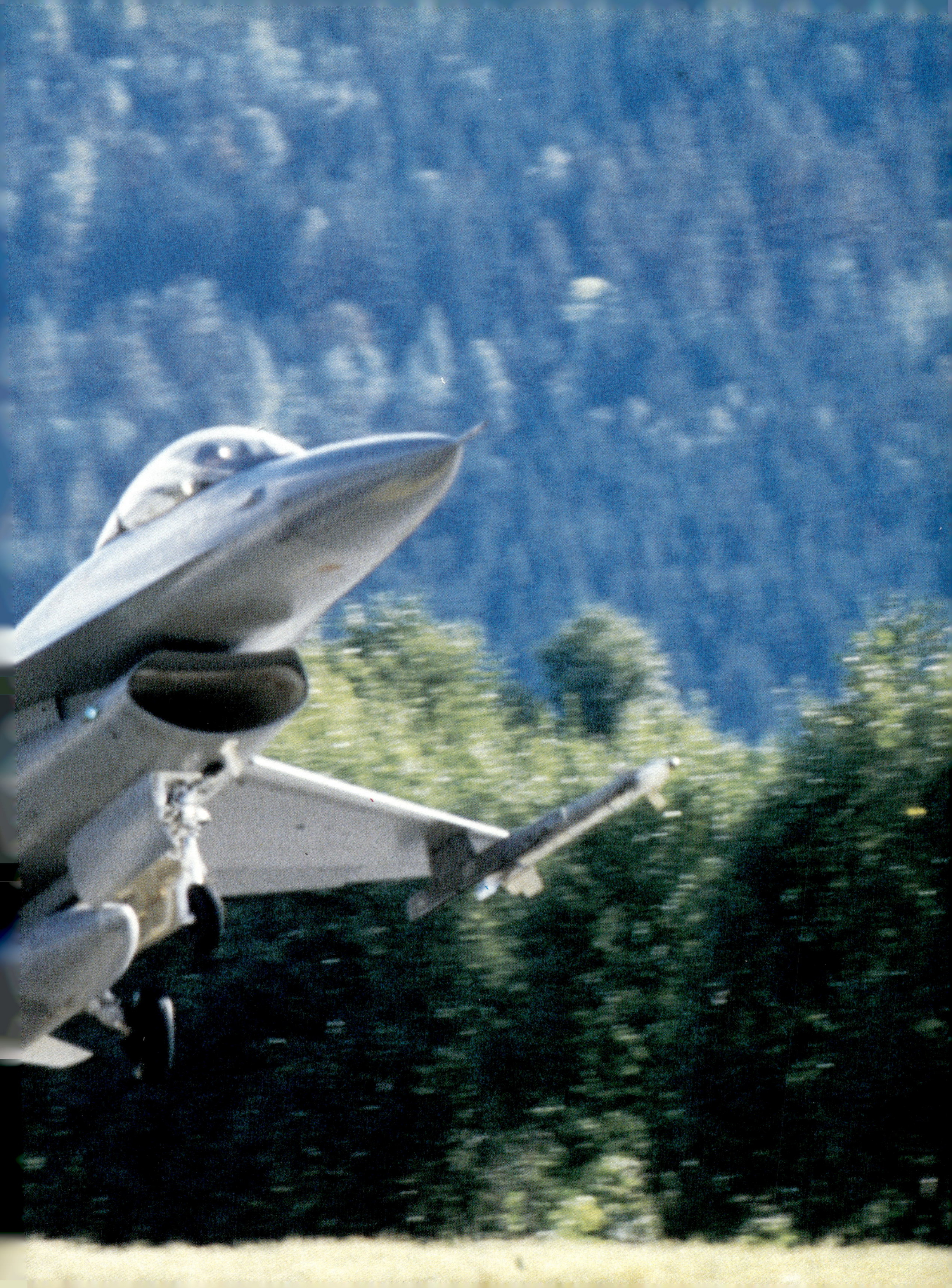

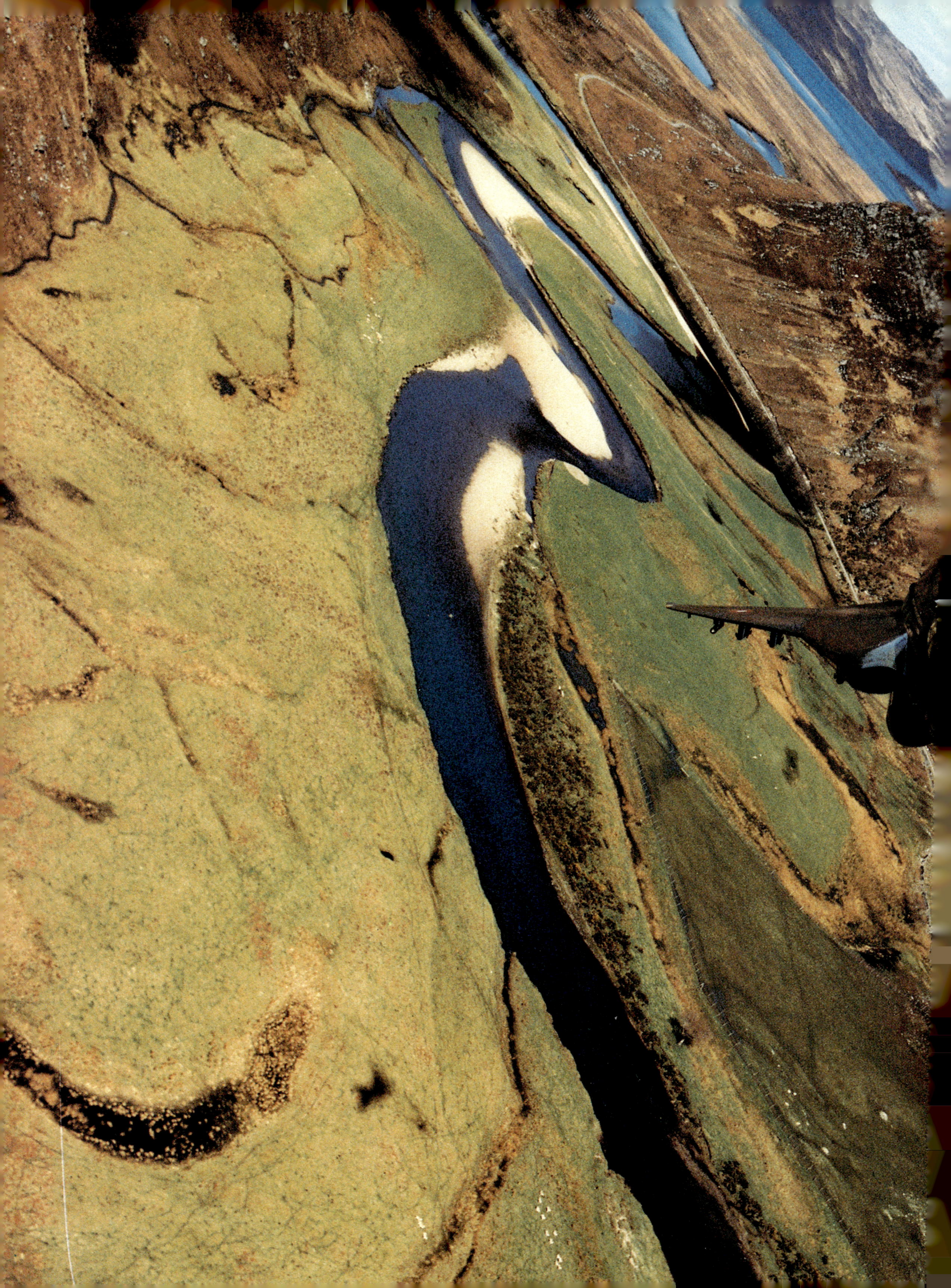

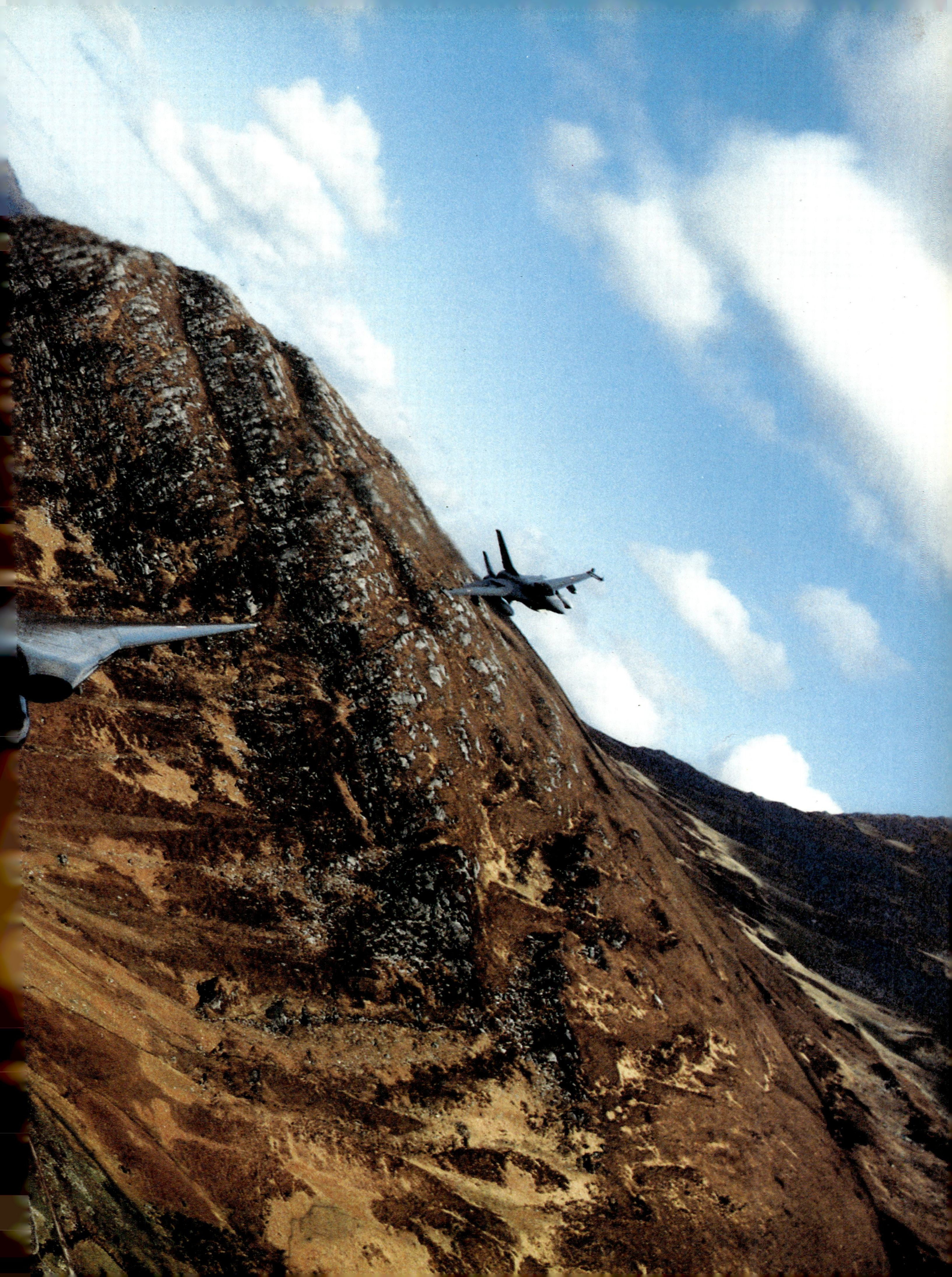

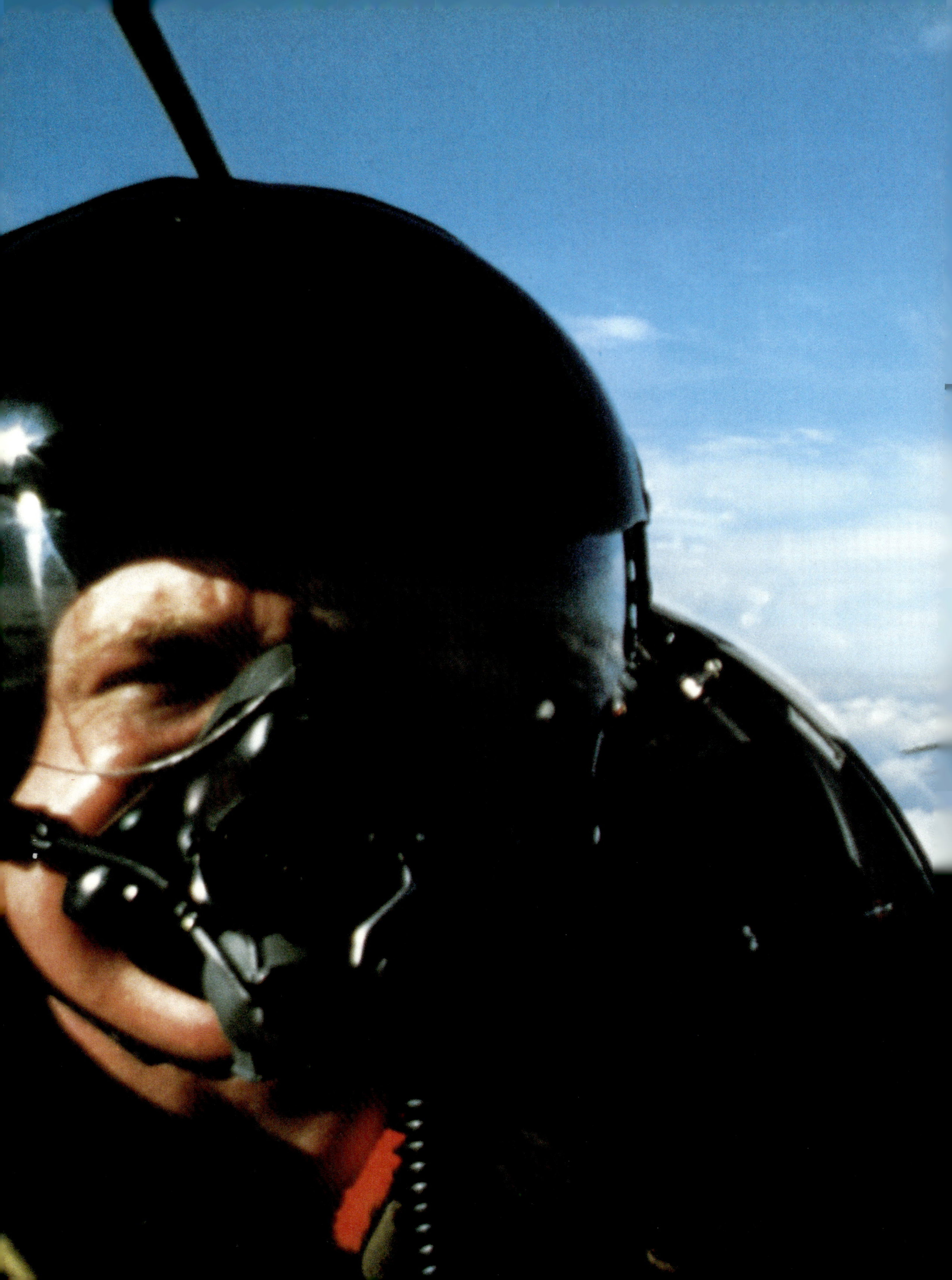

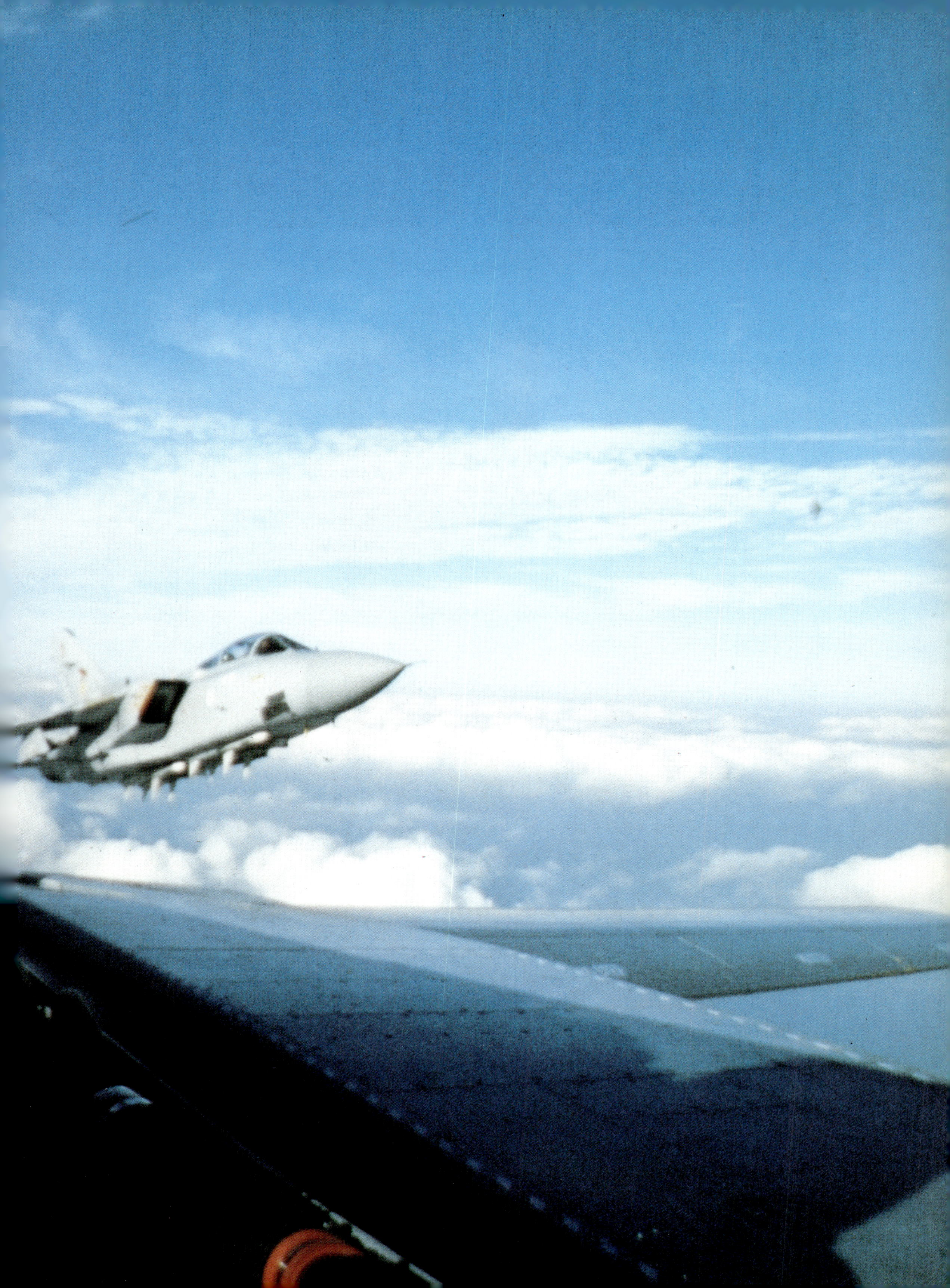

Copyright © Carl Bjerredahl 1989

First published in Denmark in 1989 by Jetpress, Anpartsselskab, Dr. Tvaergade 58, Copenhagen, Denmark.

English language edition first published in 1990 by
Airlife Publishing Ltd., 101 Longden Road, Shrewsbury SY3 9EB, England.

ISBN 1 85310 146 X

British Library Cataloguing in Publication Data available.

All rights reserved. No part of this book may be reproduced or transmitted in any form or by any means, electronic or mechanical including photocopying, recording or by any information storage and retrieval system, without permission from the Publisher in writing.

Airlife Publishing Ltd.
101 Longden Road, Shrewsbury SY3 9EB, England

KNIGHTS OF THE SKY is first and foremost a pictorial book. Its pictures, which might well comprise one of the best collections of aviation photography to be found, will take the reader into the heart of the fighter pilots' daily routine.

Aerial photography of high performance aircraft often produces breath-taking results, but it is among the toughest challenges a photographer can face.

Because of this, putting together a book of this nature was always exciting but never easy. A great deal is owed to the pilots who took their cameras with them and brought back a piece of their world to share with us. A similar debt is owed to the technicians who maintained the jets which they flew.

We owe many more a great deal for their contributions. Among them: Saab-Scandia, the Royal Air Force, British Aerospace, the Royal Danish Air Force, the Royal Norwegian Air Force, the Swedish Air Force, and the United States Air Force. Most of all, thanks to the many, they know who they are, who would rather make room for an extra picture than see their names here.

Less than a century ago, the Wright brothers took the first step towards the skies. This book is dedicated to those who took up the challenge.

C.B.

KNIGHTS OF THE SKY

CARL BJERREDAHL
AND CAPTAIN JON CASELLO
FIGHTER PILOT

Airlife
England

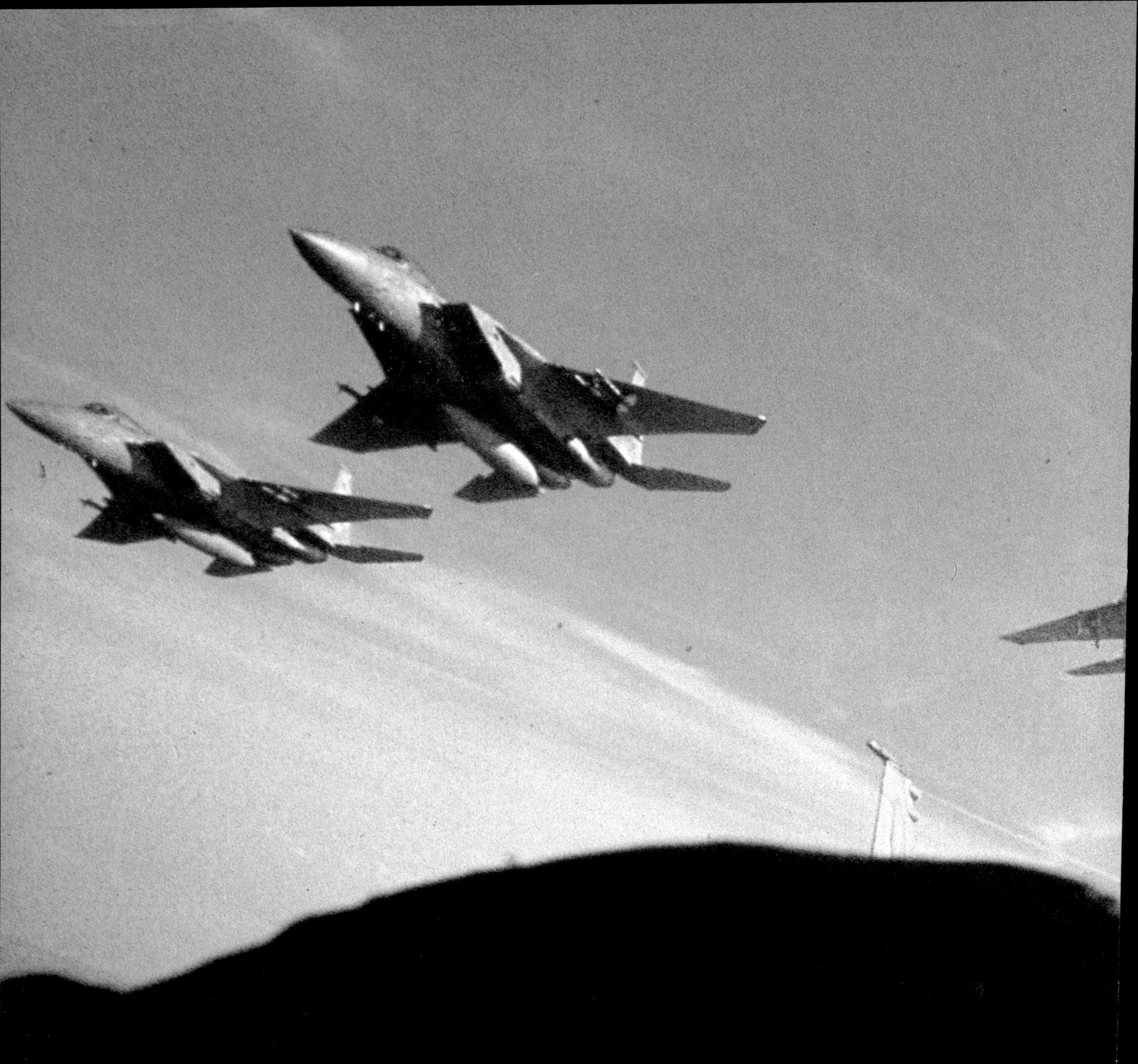

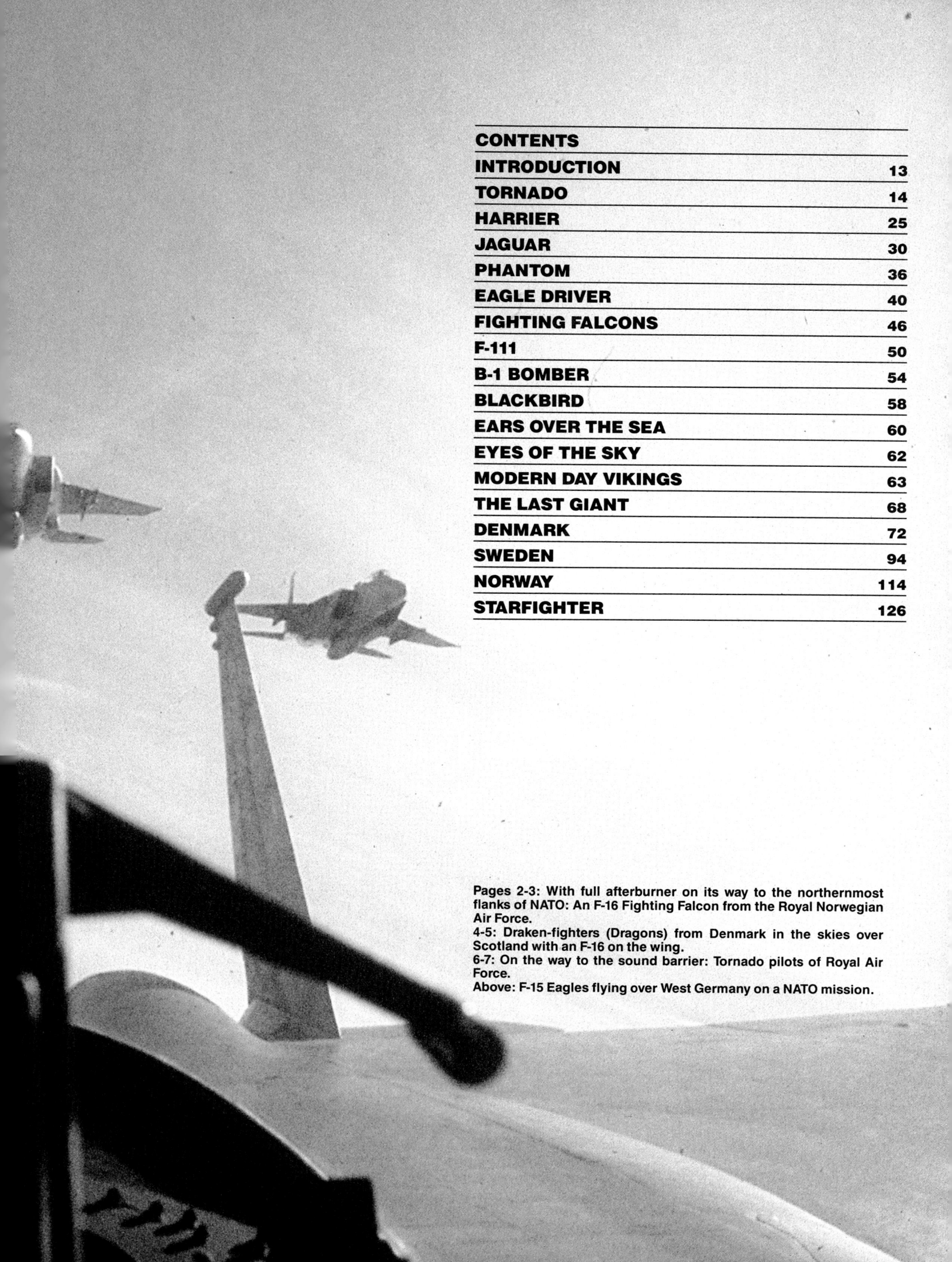

CONTENTS	
INTRODUCTION	13
TORNADO	14
HARRIER	25
JAGUAR	30
PHANTOM	36
EAGLE DRIVER	40
FIGHTING FALCONS	46
F-111	50
B-1 BOMBER	54
BLACKBIRD	58
EARS OVER THE SEA	60
EYES OF THE SKY	62
MODERN DAY VIKINGS	63
THE LAST GIANT	68
DENMARK	72
SWEDEN	94
NORWAY	114
STARFIGHTER	126

Pages 2-3: With full afterburner on its way to the northernmost flanks of NATO: An F-16 Fighting Falcon from the Royal Norwegian Air Force.
4-5: Draken-fighters (Dragons) from Denmark in the skies over Scotland with an F-16 on the wing.
6-7: On the way to the sound barrier: Tornado pilots of Royal Air Force.
Above: F-15 Eagles flying over West Germany on a NATO mission.

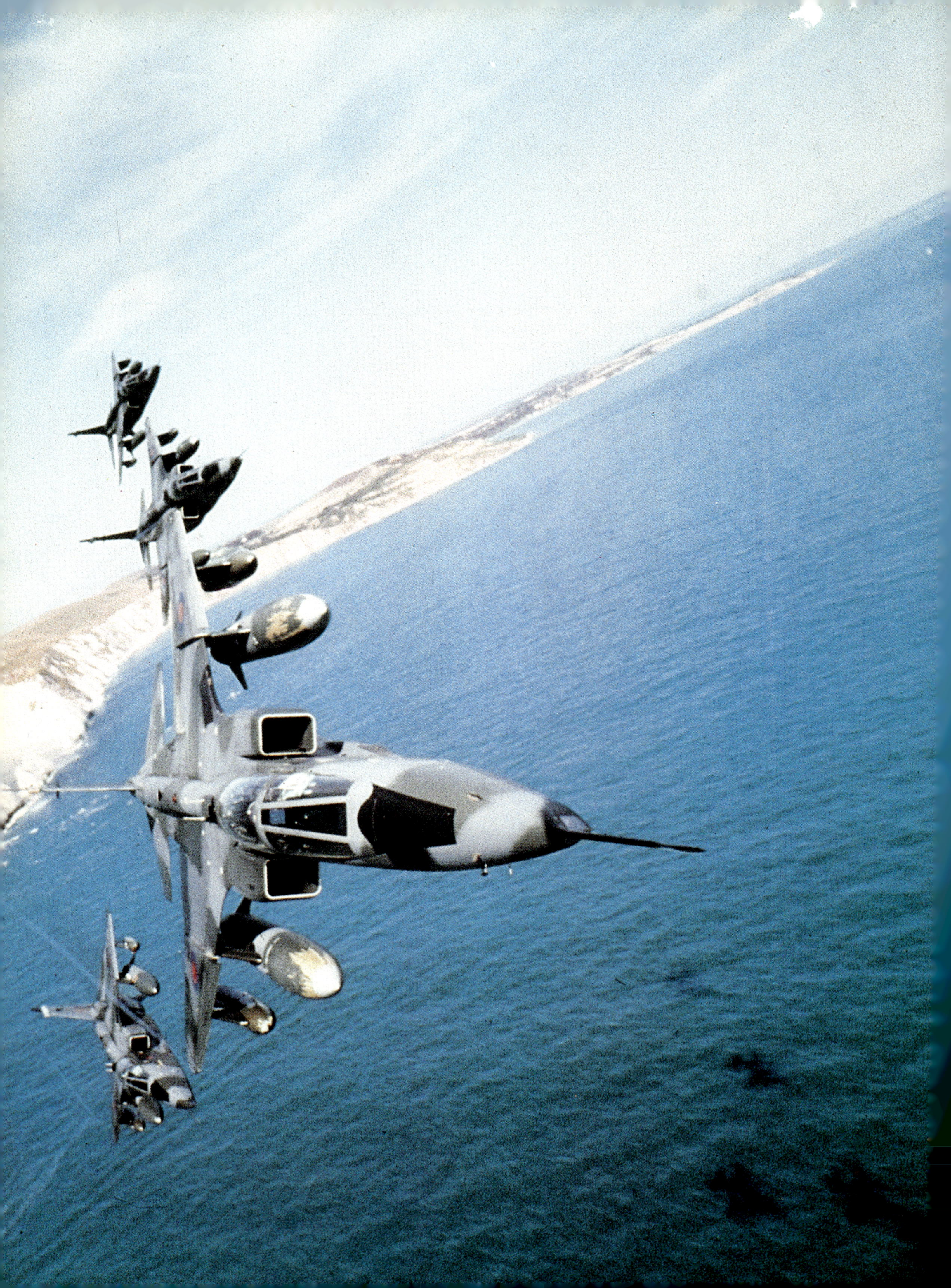

...BUT SOMEBODY JUST HAS TO DO IT!

No one will claim it is fun to be at the mercy of a terrain-following radar as you hurtle through the blackest night or the thickest weather at treetop level. There is little enjoyment in being bounced up and down in total darkness as the radar and its autopilot avoid hills, masts, and power lines which are flashing by at speeds near 650 mph. Only the radar sees them. The pilot has nothing but instruments to look at.

No one will claim it is exciting to sit alert in the cramped cockpit of an F-16 at a small airbase in a desolate part of Denmark or windblown Northern Norway well knowing that years of blood, sweat and tears can only result in one thing if the whole world goes crazy once more – he will be the one to face the most powerful war machine on earth within minutes.

No one expects that he and his fellow pilots will single-handedly defeat these superior forces; they will simply attempt to detain them. This they guarantee with their lives.

We never really think about the young American F-15 jock stationed so close to the border between East and West Germany. This border, over which NATO came into existence, is easily overflown faster than a radar controller can scramble alert pilots in their F-15s, Tornados, and Harriers.

We wouldn't think it much fun to sit in a jet for 18 hours, tracing endless circles in the sky on the odd chance that we would see the radar contact nobody ever wants to see.

But like the Americans say: Someone just has to do it! And they do it. From Northern Norway's fjords, over Sweden's large forests and Denmark's farmland; from the southern edges of West Germany and the farthest corners of Scotland has come a gathering of warriors who have been forced to live with the realities of war for thousands of years and will do almost anything to avoid a new one. This book concentrates exclusively on those that guard Northern Europe and, indirectly, the skies over the free world: the modern knights and their machines. Here in Northern Europe a fighter pilot lives an extremely low-keyed existence in comparison with those in the USA. Here there are no idols à la *Top Gun*. A fighter pilot doesn't talk very much about his job because for many he stands for the large scale consumption of taxpayers' money. In countries like West Germany his daily low level training flights are an abomination to many. They are seldom photographed because the very tools of their trade have come to symbolize death and destruction.

Their mission is to prevent exactly that.

In spite of the odds against them, in spite of the difference in cultures, language, and training, the fighter pilots of NATO and Sweden have earned enormous respect the world over. Year after year they fight to be among the very best. Their ancestors did the same. From Norway's Vikings who sailed the Atlantic 1000 years ago; from Denmark and Sweden's 1000-year-old monarchies; from England's Knights of the Round Table; and from the legendary Red Baron...

The spirit is alive...

"Coming from the Phantom to the Tornado is like switching from a youth hostel to the Hilton. I'm a pretty fair-sized guy, hell, I have to squeeze myself into an F-16. The cockpit seems so small I think I would get claustrophobic if I had to fly one. To me, flying fighters is a job. So why should my office be any less comfortable than the other guy's? Just give me a Tornado and a good back-seater and the other guy will have to get up pretty damn early in the morning to have much of a chance tangling with us."

The Tornado, together with the F-15 and F-16 form the front line of defense on NATO's northern flank. The design and construction of this two-seat, supersonic fighter was the result of a joint effort between three countries: Britain, West Germany, and Italy. Today, the swing-winged Tornado comprises a major portion of each country's defense. The Tornado, which first flew operationally in 1982, has been the envy of other pilots ever since. In many respects, the Tornado has parallelled the American F-14 Tomcat: both have a pilot and navigator (called an RIO, radar intercept officer, in the Tomcat); both are swing-winged, twin engined fighters and are capable of supersonic flight. The Tomcat, however, operates primarily from aircraft carriers while its European counterpart prefers solid ground. Back to the RAF lieutenant and his description of a day in the life of a Tornado pilot.

"The cockpit is very roomy in comparison with other jets, and the noise level is not unlike that of a commercial airliner. We primarily fly on 'high-low-high' training missions. The turnpoints for the entire mission are recorded on a cassette-like tape prior to the mission which is then loaded into the Tornado's main computer. We are off the ground at 150 knots and then climb to our initial cruise altitude of 30,000 feet. Coupled to the pre-loaded turn points, the autopilot can guide the aircraft over the majority of the mission. In fact, if I chose to use the autopilot to the fullest of its capabilities, there is very little I would have to do before landing again.

"Long before we enter the target area we drop down into the low level environment – 200 feet at 480 knots. The autopilot is then tied in with the TFR (terrain following radar) which guides the Tornado over obstacles along its route. Although the system is extremely reliable, the pilot's eyes seldom stray long from the TFR because if the TFR and its backup system fail, unbeknown to the pilot, the results can be catastrophic. The navigator in the back seat constantly updates the target position as the jet races towards the target. At this speed and altitude we have a fair chance of slipping in under the enemy's radar. The Tornado's size allows it to carry a tremendous weapon load and its systems accuracy is amazing. Once guided to the target, it can actually drop its own weapons with the pilot's consent.

"We hug the ground in an attempt to make the SAM's (surface-to-air missile) job as difficult as possible. In fact, our biggest threat now is birds. At 480 knots, a collision with a large bird is like an explosion. Fortunately, in our training areas in Britain, we know where they are – and they know us. The thunder from four Tornados in formation doesn't bother them in the least. They seem to have become used to us. It is as if we've become sort of colleagues.

(continued on page 18)

15

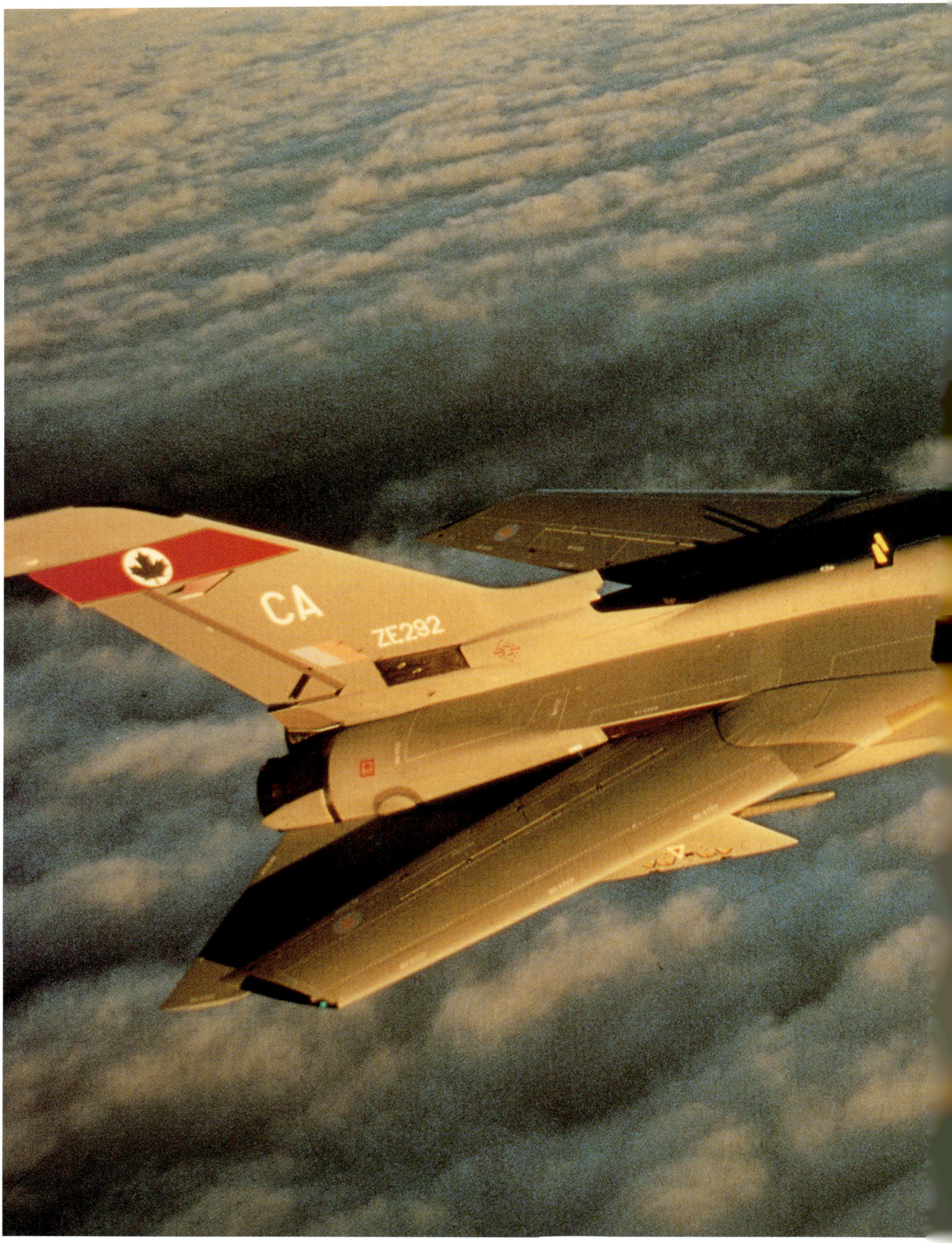
CA
ZE292

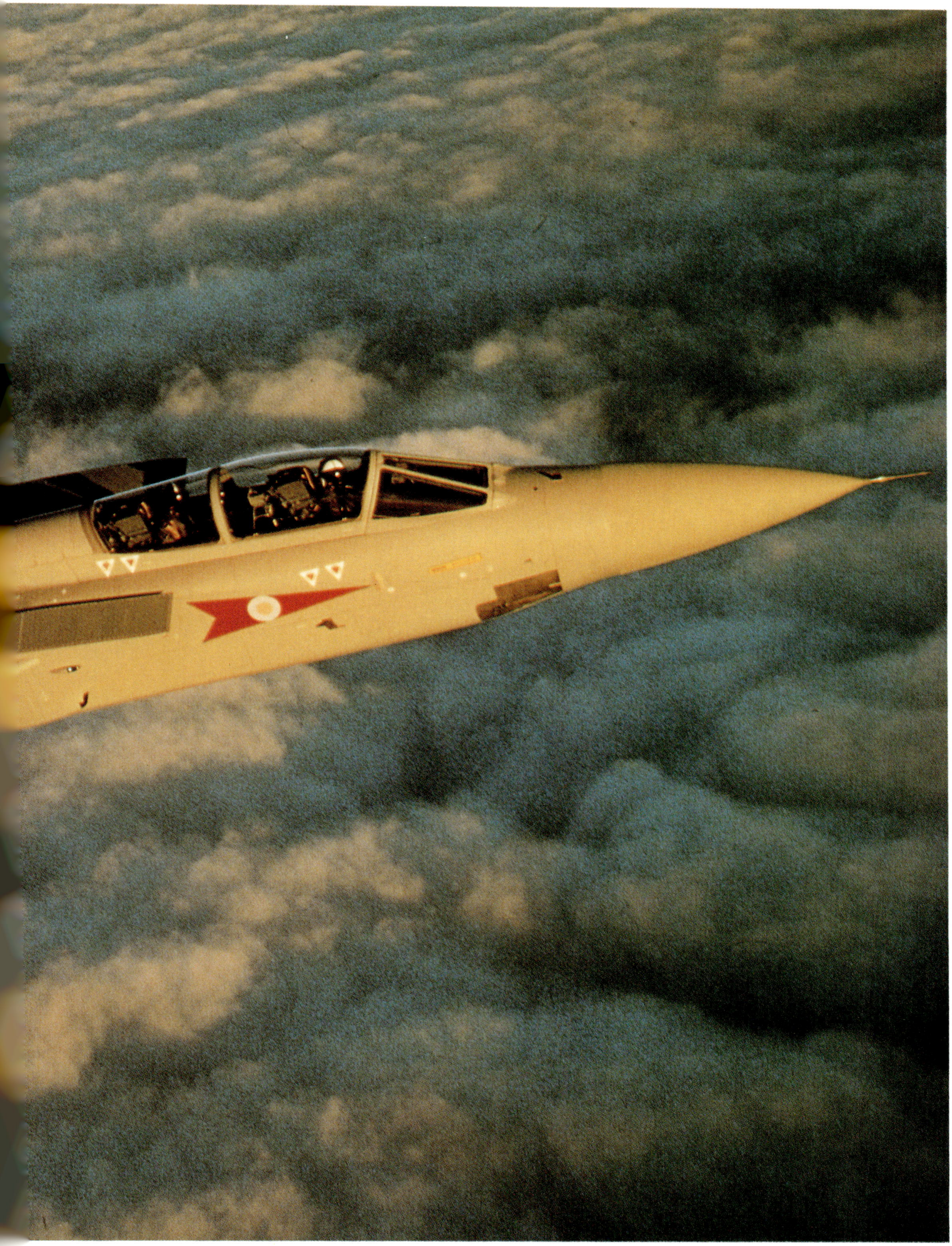

(continued from page 14)

"The Tornado was designed to succeed the F-4, which it has done very well. I think the Tornado's a sure winner every time. The only real threat to a Tornado is another modern air defense fighter. The F-16, for example, is a formidable challenge, but you really can't be sure of the outcome if we were to meet in the sky."

The Tornado is also flown by the West German Marines stationed just south of the Danish-German border. There, it has replaced the legendary F-104 Starfighter. Although the Starfighter is totally antiquated by today's technology, it is one of the few jets which could give the Tornado a good fight.

19

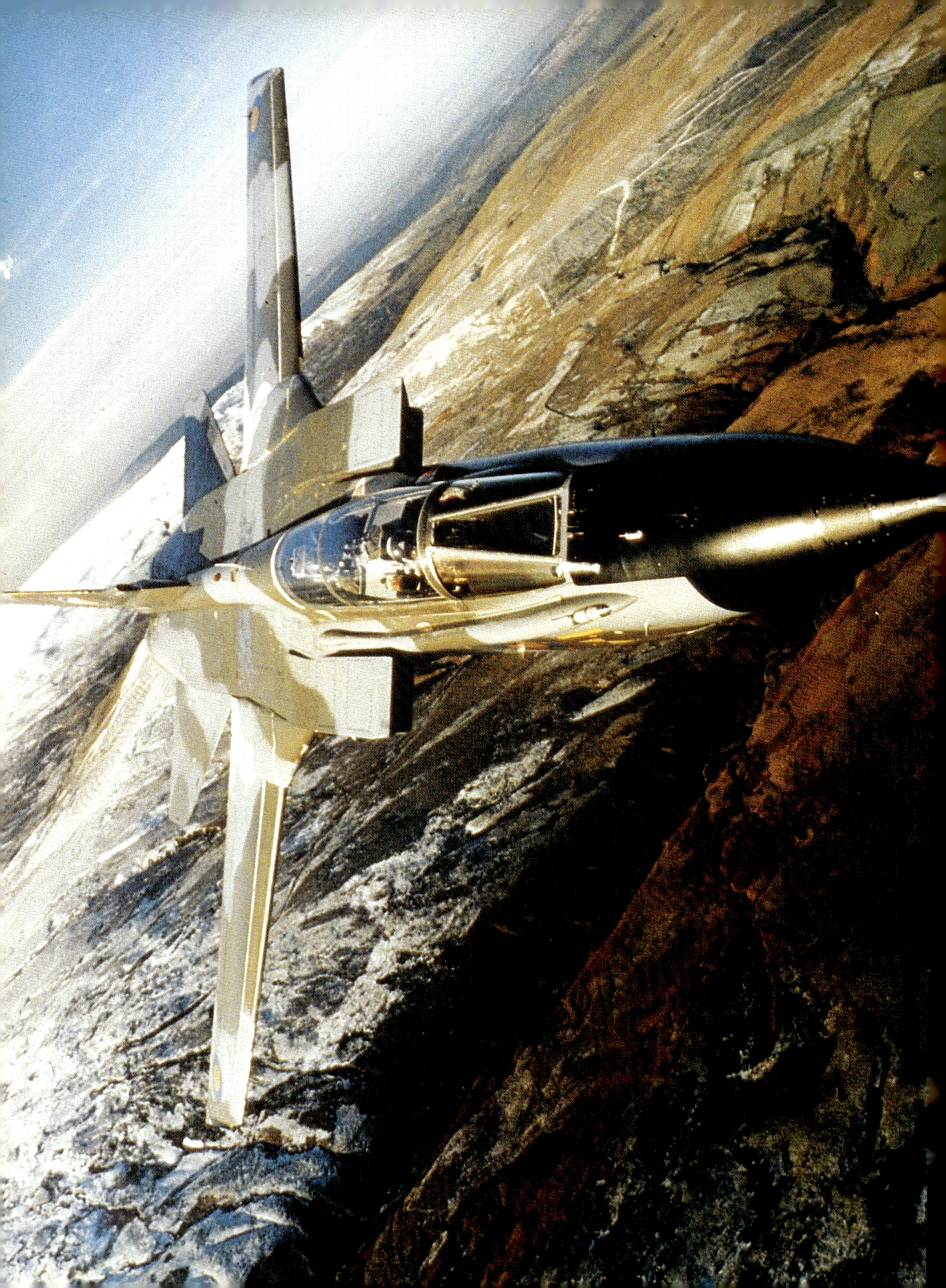

The Tornado can be fitted out with a variety of weapons of which the Sky Flash air-to-air missile has proved itself to be one of the most reliable. The Royal Air Force maintains its accuracy runs as high as 85%. Here the radar-guided Sky Flash is fired from a Tornado and races towards its target at over Mach 4.

The bridge, the very mention of whose name can still kindle the fires of rage in the hearts of the British, and whose construction cost the lives of so many prisoners of war: The Bridge over the River Kwai. Above the bridge flies an RAF Tornado F3 from 29 Squadron which had deployed from its home base in England to participate in an exercise over Thailand.

Britain's fighters can now be found sweeping the skies over its old colony of Singapore where this new Tornado F3 has slowed down to just 170 knots for a photograph.

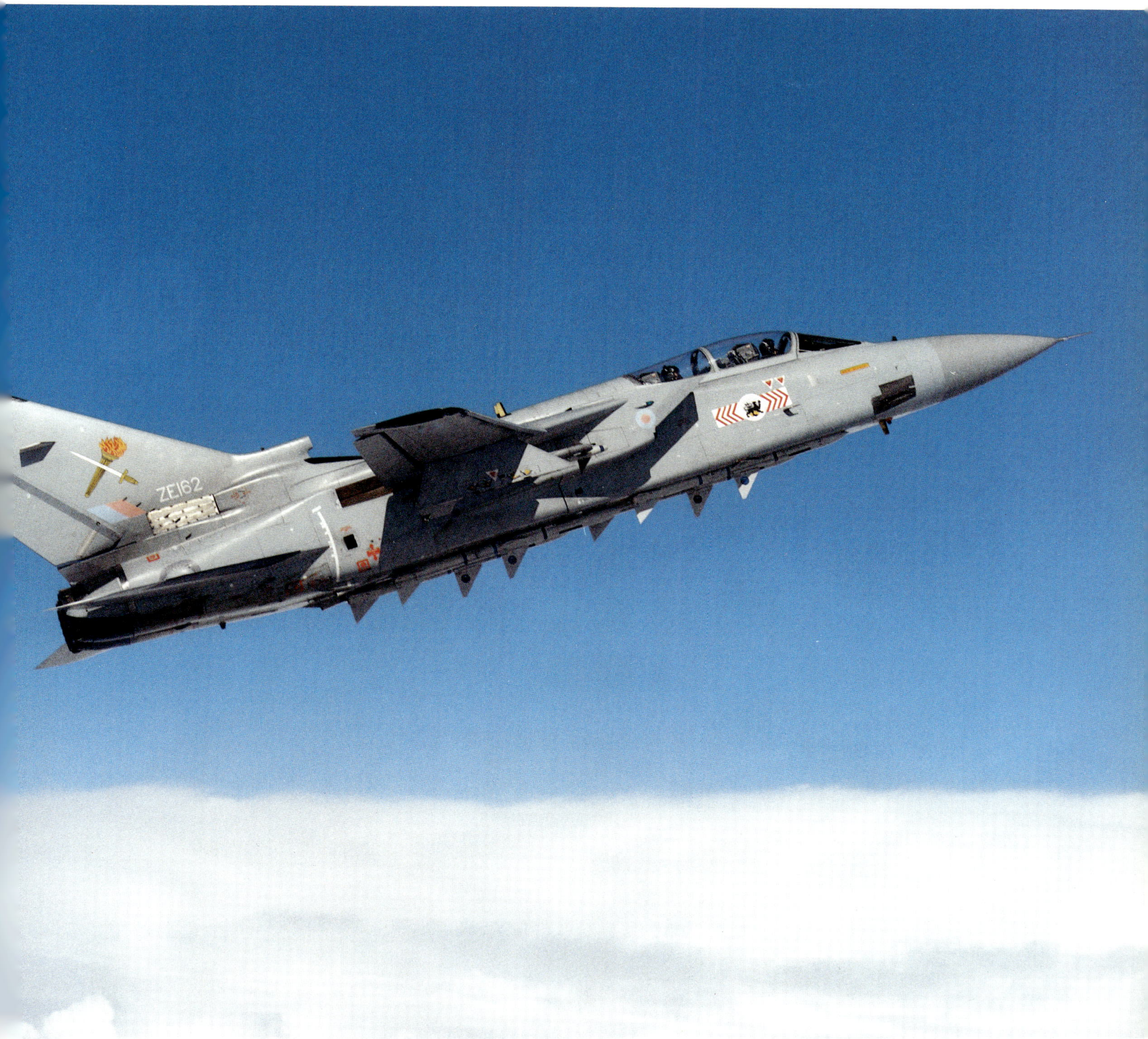

The world seen from a Tornado pilot's point of view. Flight Lieutenant Tony Paxton flies Tornado F3s for the Royal Air Force's 29 Squadron based out of Leeming, England. Normally his seat is in front as the pilot, but here he has taken the radar officer's back seat to get these photos. Above, his Tornado flies in tight formation with another F3. To the right is the radar officer's instrument panel, while another Tornado flies ahead to the left. (Because of the somewhat cramped quarters, the only way this picture of both crew members and the other F3 could be taken was by taping the camera to the top of the rear ejection seat.)

- It is better to stop and land than to land and have to stop!
- If it wasn't for the Sea Harriers, I'm afraid Britain would have lost the Falkland War.
- In the new Harrier GR5, the entire weapons system is hands-on. Gone are the days of having to look inside to find the right switch and in so doing taking my eyes off the guy trying to kill me. With the new weapon systems I only need one pass. There won't be any need for a second shot. We finish the job the first time round.

The new jet fighter, which few people thought would ever get off the ground, has earned excellent reviews from all who have flown it. The British Aerospace Harrier has come a long way since the joint project to improve its capabilities was entered into between Britain and the USA. The latest product of this co-operative effort was released as the Harrier GR5 or, in the case of the US Marine version, the AV-8B. This new Harrier, possibly the world's most unusual fighter, will, together with its predecessor, the GR3, stand guard on the borders between East and West in a constant state of readiness. Its remarkable and unique capabilities may allow it to operate when others have been rendered useless.

The Harrier is a V/STOL fighter, a sort of cross between a jet and a helicopter. Outwardly, it appears to be just another fighter – mean and nasty. But the similarities end as it makes a vertical takeoff which any helicopter would be proud of. After a mission which it has flown as a fighter, it will return and land once again exactly like a helicopter, independent of any prepared runway. To better understand the truly amazing capabilities of this fighter, we strap in behind an RAF pilot in his Harrier GR3 stationed at RAF Gutersloh close to the border between East and West Germany.

"The Harrier's strength lies in its ability to strike quickly. There is no need for a long trip over friendly territory prior to ingressing towards the target. The Harrier is already prepositioned at forward operating areas close to the battle zone; able to move quickly to where the action is. We support the ground forces primarily by clearing their way of enemy tanks, but we can also hold off enemy fighters should the need arise. With the Harrier's VIFF (Vectoring In Forward Flight) system, we can make the jet literally dance in close combat which will wreak havoc on even the Soviets' new Su-27 Flanker and MiG-29 Fulcrum.

A Harrier is foremost an attack aircraft, which was designed to take out ground targets in support of ground troops, while fighters like the F-15 or F-16 fly cover above. The new Harrier GR5 is so advanced, however, it can actually operate as its own fighter cover. This was effectively proven in the Falkland War, where the small Harriers fared quite well against the Argentinean fighters.

(continued on next page)

(continued)

"The Harrier lifts off when I vector the thrust downward. The throttle and nozzle controls are combined and I set them in 'Hover stop'. I have already been through the checklist and set my flaps. I push the throttle up to full power and the Harrier is airborne. It is so easy. Safely away from the ground, I retract my gear and flaps. By shifting the direction in which the nozzles are vectoring the thrust, we slowly transition from a hover to forward flight. In under 20 seconds, I am at a safe altitude with 180 knots on the clock – what we call 'safe speed'. The whole process uses a tenth of the fuel an F-4 burns to get airborne.

The Harrier can now be employed like an ordinary fighter, but it still has the advantage of its V/STOL capabilities. We call it VIFF – vectoring in forward flight. This system was developed by the US Marines in their version of the Harrier. The ability to literally stop in the air, turn around and fire can be an enormous advantage in a dogfight. The only catch is that you may then be an easy target for your adversary's wingman. Personally I don't think the system is necessary, but every pilot must decide that for himself.

"The Harrier is a front line fighter which operates initially from extremely vulnerable bases. Because of this, we fully expect our bases to be rendered unusable in the conventional sense long before we turn for home. To an ordinary fighter this presents three rather distressing possibilities: find another base, which may also be destroyed; find a piece of highway he can use; or eject. The Harriers, however, have a large number of secret landing zones. We can seemingly disappear into the forest if we choose. The location of these landing zones is changing all the time. A specially trained ground crew can have us airborne again in 30 minutes. We can be back where the action is in a heartbeat. When that mission is finished, it's back to another secret base. In fact, the biggest problem with this system is finding the landing zones which are so camouflaged you practically need an infrared radar to find the planes.

"Over the landing site I reverse the thrust vectoring process and the Harrier gently lets down. In the 60s people never envisioned the Harrier concept as a reality. Today, the question is whether or not we have developed the fighter of the future.

(continued on page 28)

27

(continued)

"The Harriers' success in the Falkland War greatly accented the uniqueness of the fighter. The GR5 contains state of the art avionics, in many cases using the same equipment which made the McDonnel Douglas F-18 Hornet one of the world's most advanced fighters on the other side of the sound barrier. The Royal Air Force's most important Harrier squadrons are stationed in West Germany allowing them quick access to the border between NATO and Warsaw Pact nations. The Royal Navy uses the Sea Harrier version on their carriers. The US Marines, which have been through all types of fighters, are extremely pleased with the strength and versatility of this V/STOL fighter. With its ability to strike quickly and be effective in support of ground troops, it would have proved indispensible during the Vietnam War."

– *Harrier Pilot, RAF*

Page 27: *A Harrier GR3 demonstrates its vertical takeoff ability – a dramatic sight with a Scottish city in the background. A vertical takeoff is impressive, and also very noisy. A Harrier is in the same noise class as a 1950s jet.*

Seen on the bottom of page 26 is a pilot from the US Marines that has just landed from a training mission. His Harrier version is called the AV-8B and is the answer to the new Harrier GR5 seen above and to the right.

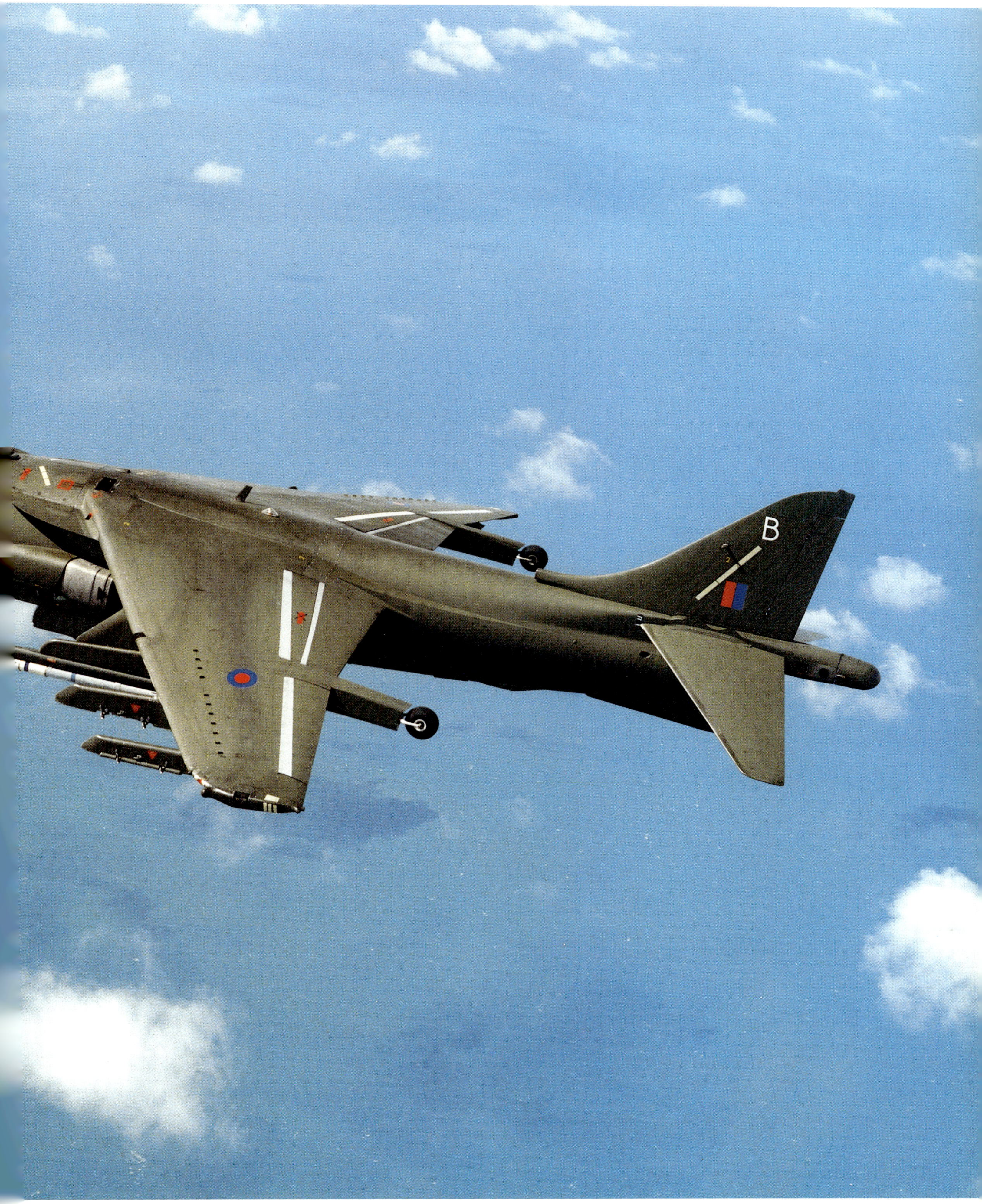
B

Few military planes have had so thankless a lot as the streamlined Jaguar. The Jaguar was built as a joint effort between France and Britain, but seldom have the classic differences between the two countries appeared more evident. There were major disagreements about everything and, as a result, the Jaguar was produced in two completely different versions. Time was critical in the development of the Jaguar: the British needed it to help meet the demand created by the phasing out of the Vulcan bombers and the Canberras, while the French needed it to cover the gap in the country's Mirage development. There are those who believe the Jaguar's full potential was never realized because of this lack of unity in effort. Nevertheless, the supersonic fighter has performed well in one of the world's most challenging fighter exercises – Red Flag held at Nellis AFB in the USA. Here the fighter-bomber fared well against the F-5s of the USAF Aggressors (a collection of extremely talented fighter pilots who have been assembled into a group and are dedicated to making other fighter pilots' lives hell). Today the Jaguar's role is first and foremost offensive in nature. From their bases next to the Iron Curtain, they can easily be sent deep into the East where there will no doubt be more than one MiG-21 sent to stop them. Against such a threat the Jaguar can take advantage of its low altitude supersonic capability to push through to its target.

Gradually, most of the Jaguar squadrons will be converted to the Tornado. Looking back, in view of the unforseen problems between France and Britain during its development, the Jag' has done amazingly well in living up to its powerful name.

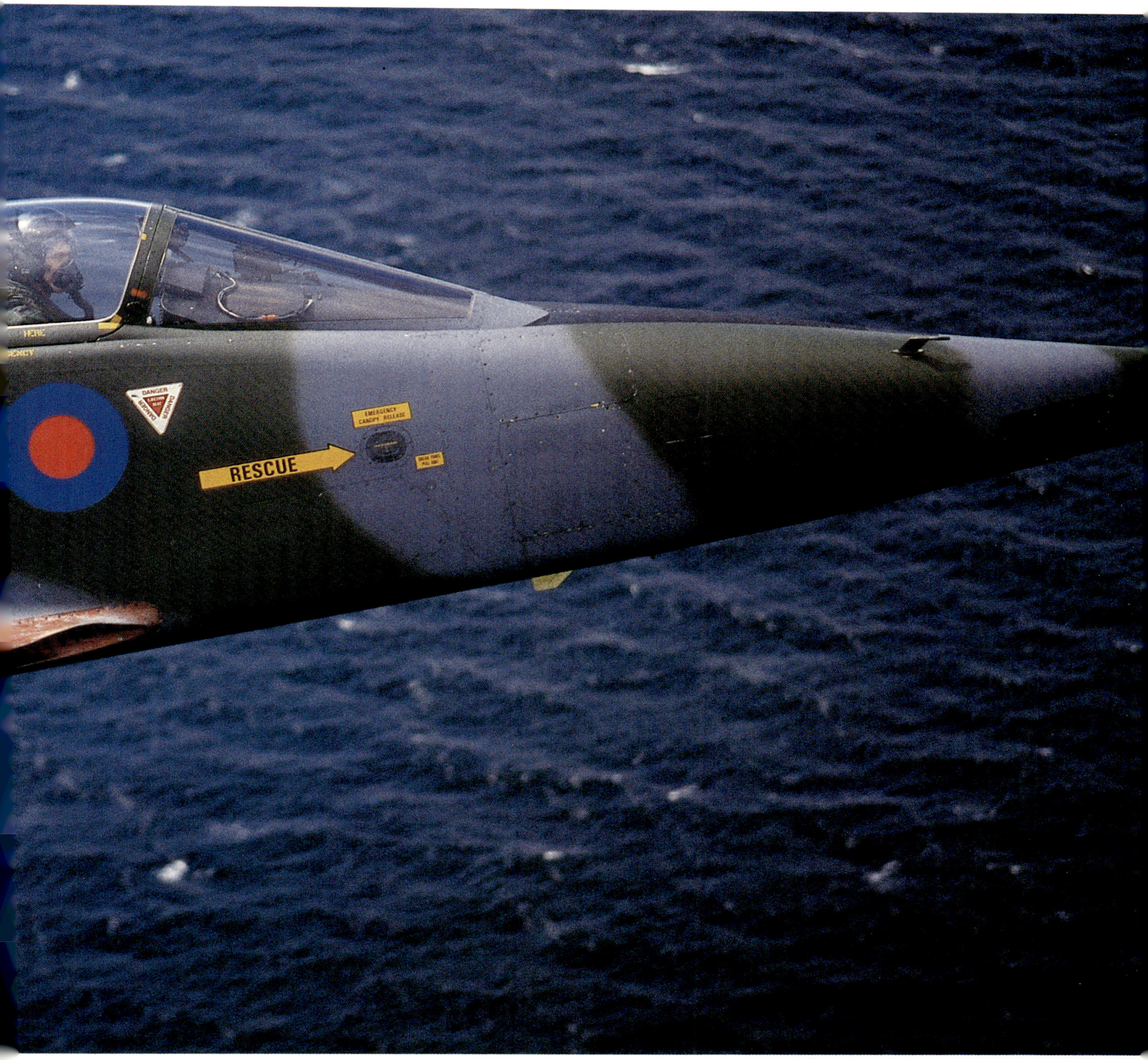
EMERGENCY
CANOPY RELEASE
RESCUE
DANGER

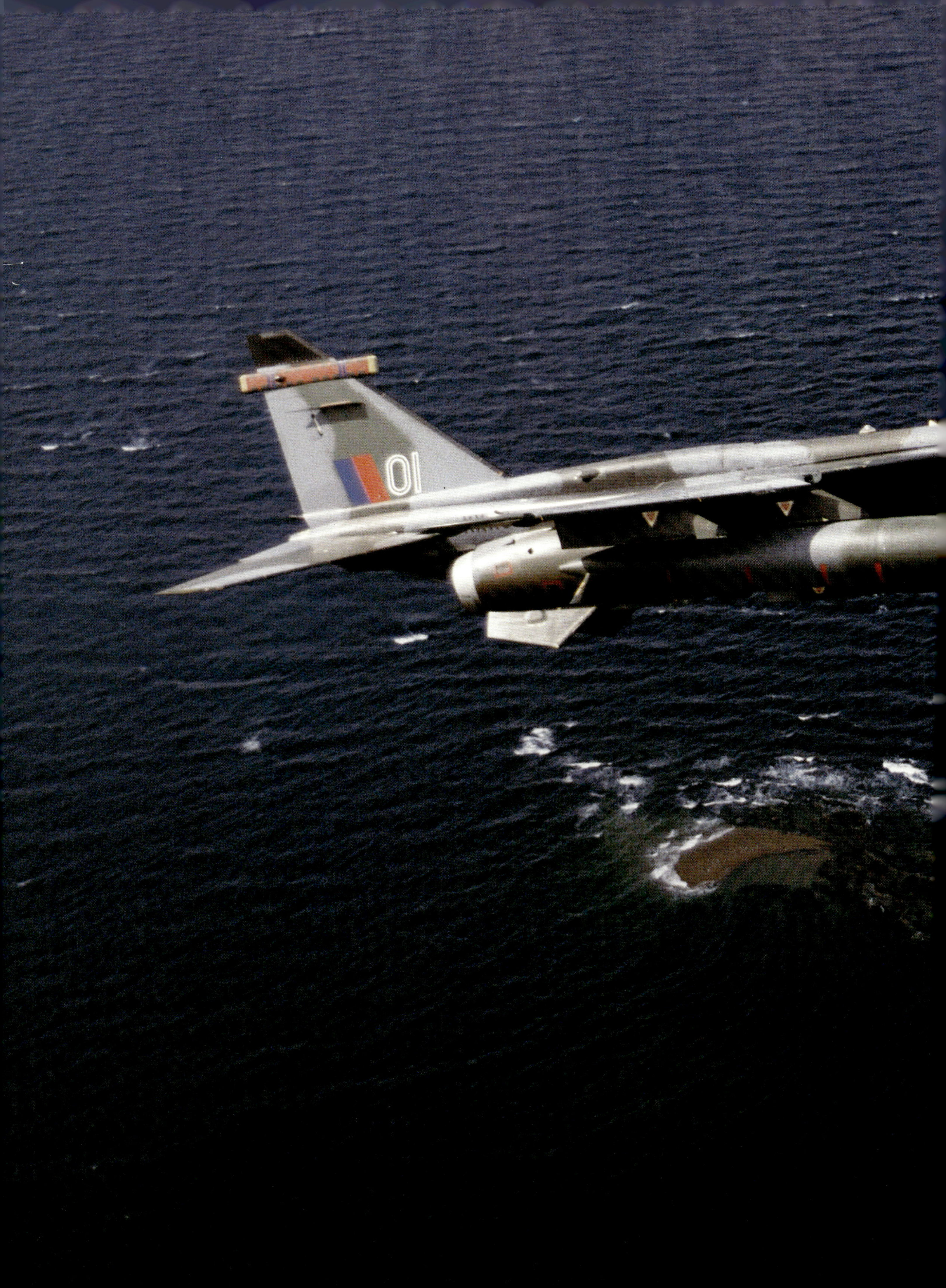
01

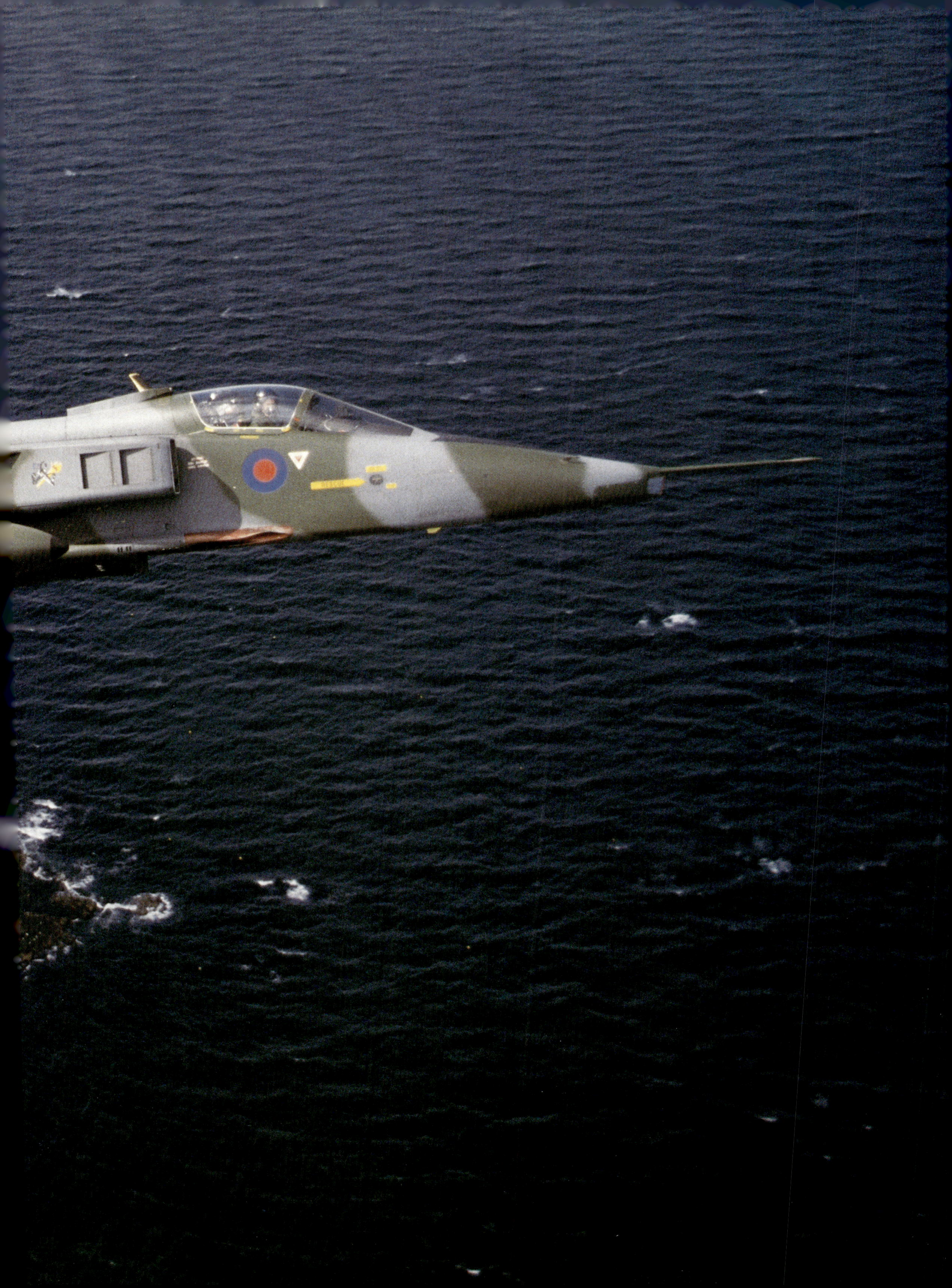

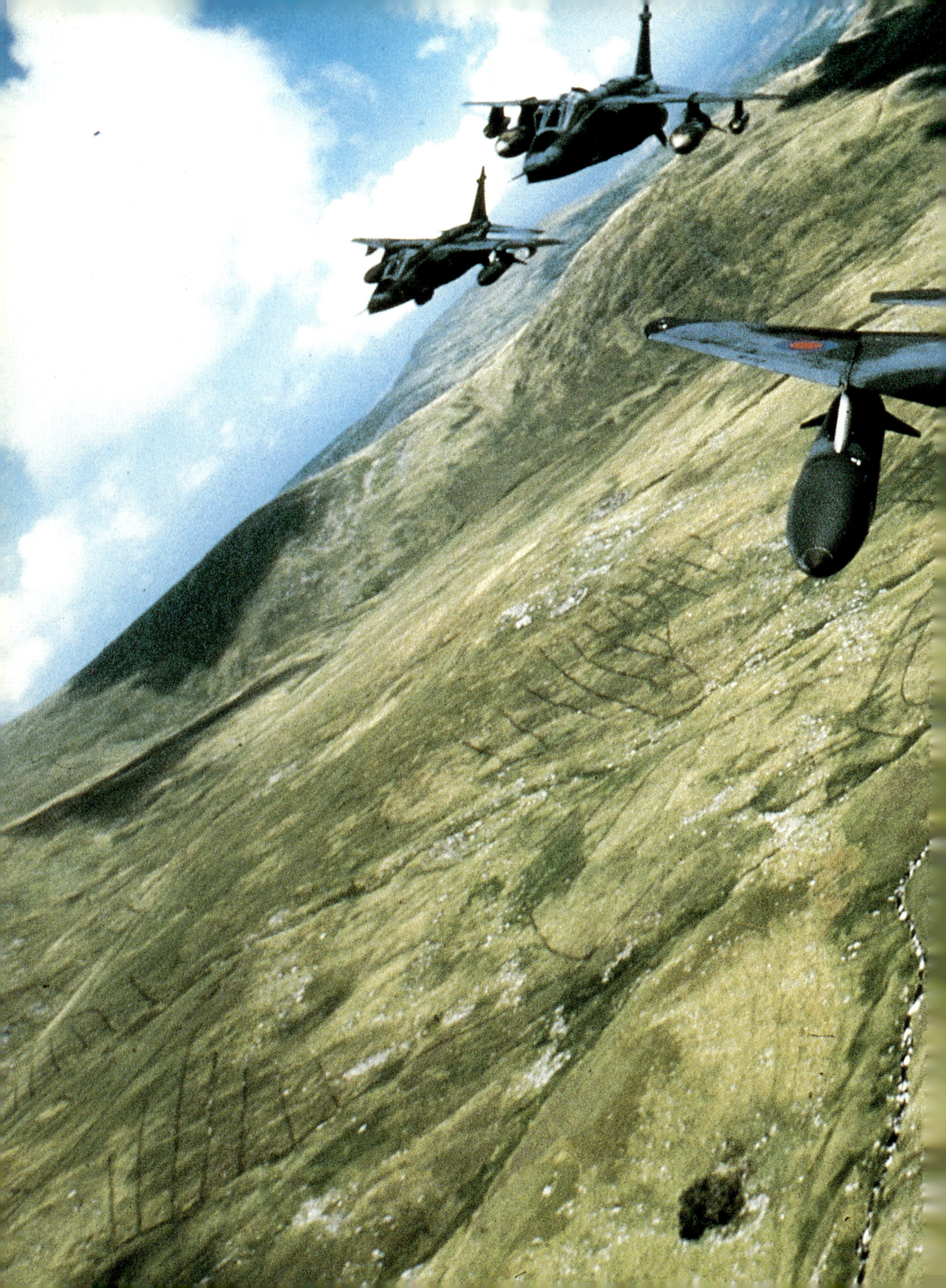

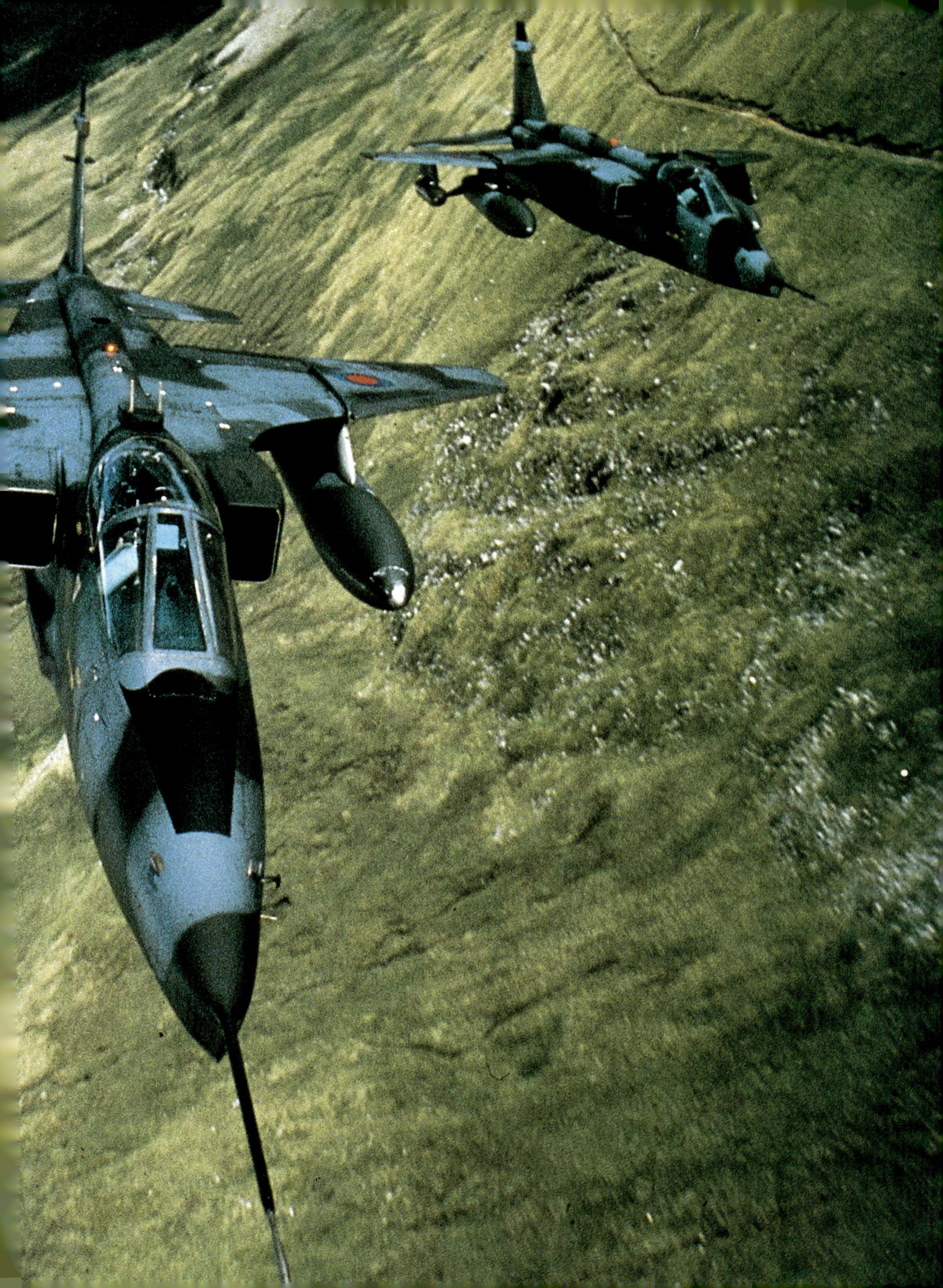

PHANTOM OF THE SKY

"I have had students that were disappointed checking out in the F-4. They had always dreamt about flying the F-15, F-111 or maybe the F-16. The F-4 is just an old bucket, they thought, close to being finished. I have to take special care with these students. When we hold at the end of the runway, I go through a special procedure with them: throttle up to 80% power standing on the brakes, release the brakes and push it up to full military; a quick check of the engine instruments as the Phantom races down the runway, and then full afterburner as we climb to 30,000 feet.

"At around 115 knots we begin to pull back on the stick, at 145 knots we are airborne. Now things begin to happen fast, faster than the speed-happy student had expected. With full afterburner, we go screaming through 30,000 as the student tries to level off. Sometimes we are as high as 40,000 before he gets her under control. It isn't him that's driving the machine, but the other way around. It's a healthy experience – he learns in hurry that the Phantom demands respect."

It was 32 years ago that the Phantom made its maiden flight. Since then, the heavy, two-seat fighter has enjoyed a long history of success without major incidents. In many ways, the Phantom has had the harshest career to date because of the large role it played in the Vietnam War. The F-4 flew for both the US Navy from carriers in the Tonkin Gulf and as the tip of the spear for the US Air Force. In Vietnam, the heavy Phantom often fought with the more manoeuverable MiGs as it protected the American strike missions. The F-4 also played an important role as the Wild Weasel. Here it was tasked to find and destroy SAM (Surface-to-Air-Missile) sites in order to clear the way for the main missions. This was possibly the most demanding mission to be flown by a fighter during the war.

Flying the Phantom is a demanding task for a pilot. It has its lighter side: cruising along with the autopilot on, enjoying the view, but all of that can disappear in a heartbeat during the course of a normal mission. Take, for example, when AWACS gives you a snap vector onto an unidentified radar contact. The twin-engine jet accelerates up to Mach 2, and the faster it goes, the tougher the jet is to control. In a modern dogfight, the Phantom doesn't always do so well, but it is a rugged machine capable of taking a lot of punishment. With the right people at the controls it can overcome quite a few shortcomings on its way to the target.

The Phantom is the "Grand Old Lady" of NATO. West Germany and Britain alone operate close to 300 F-4s in various versions. It continues to live up to its reputation as an effective, combat proven jet. In Vietnam it wasn't the planes, but the pilots that were the limiting factor at the start. Eventually, things fell into place as they learned from their mistakes and the score steadily began to rise in favor of the Phantoms. Today, years later, the Phantom remains in service over the skies of Europe, even though its successors are already flying.

"If you have the chance to rocket into space in a lightweight Phantom with the burner cooking, you'll realize how powerful it is. After a ride like that, I always tell my students to take off with military power, because that's more than enough if you're a Phantom jock..."

F-4 Pilot, USAFE

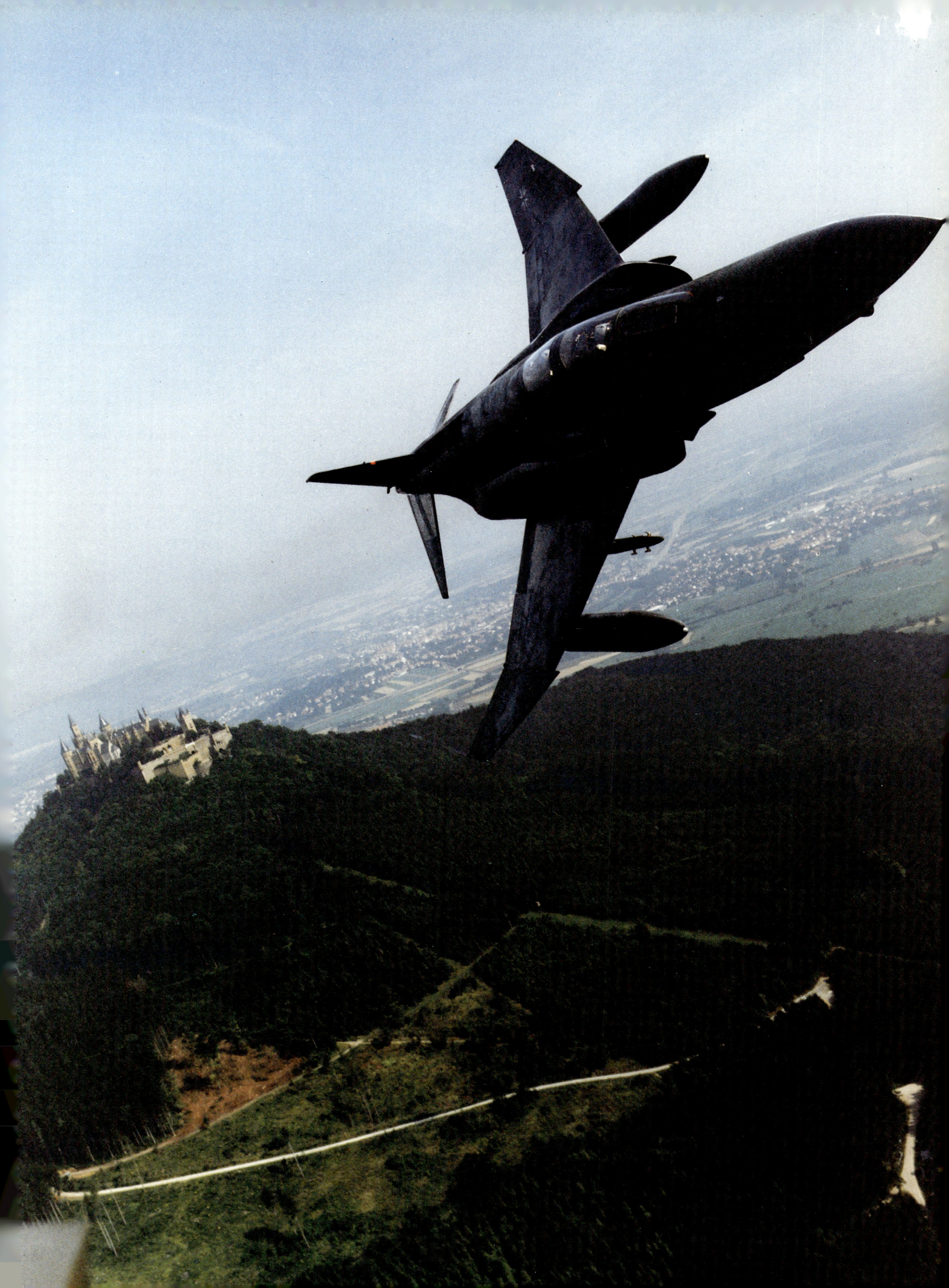

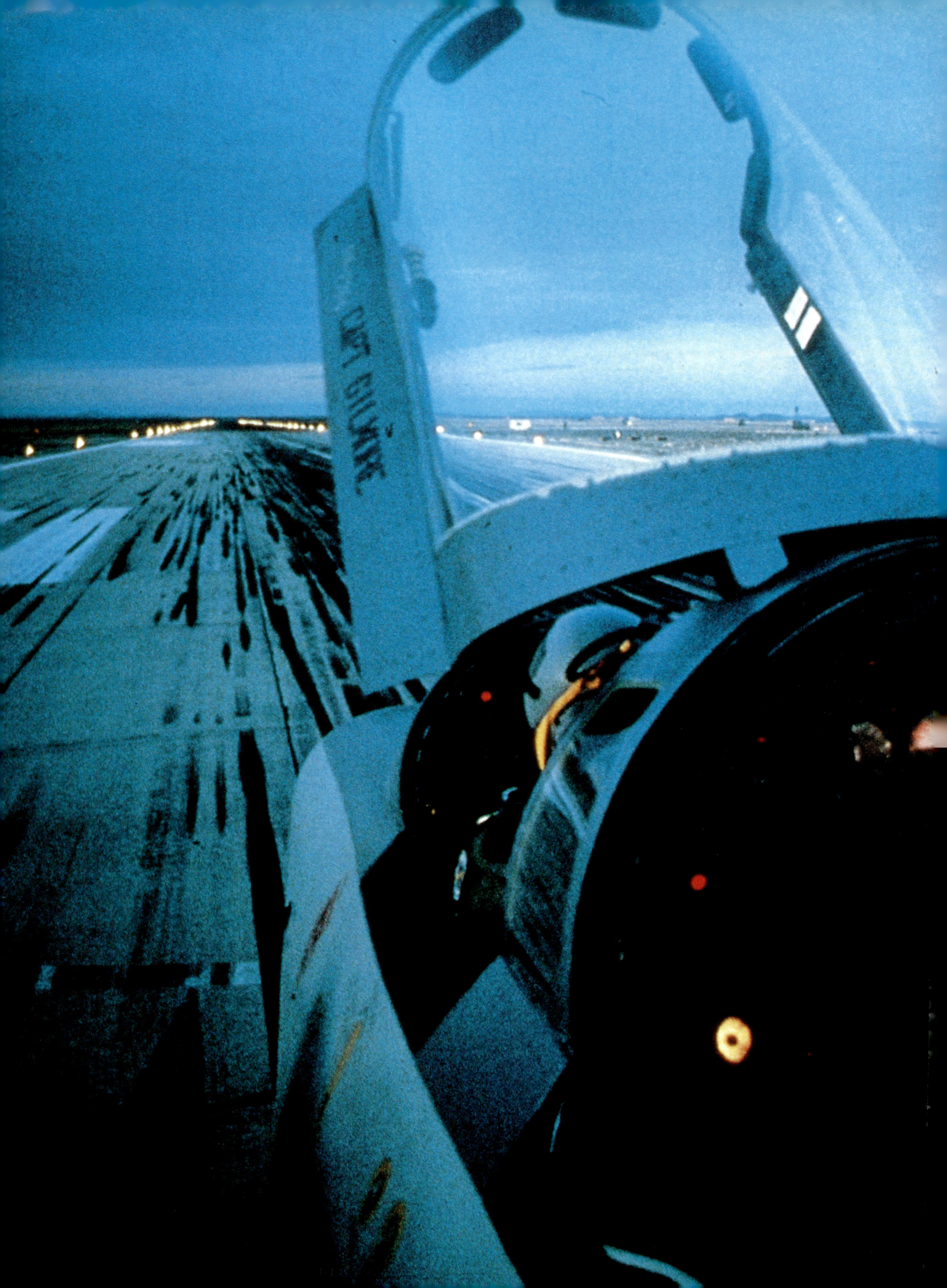

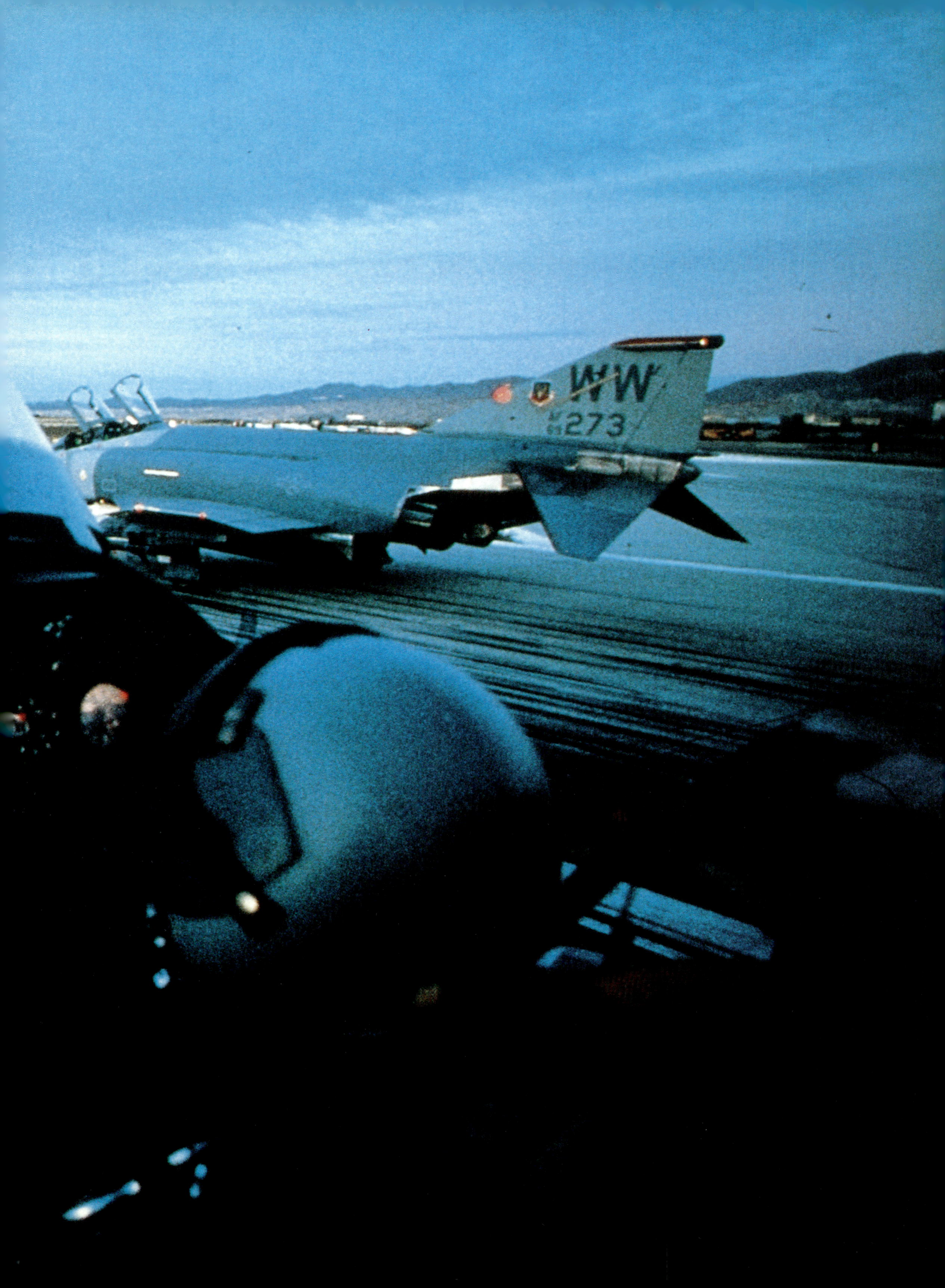
WW
273

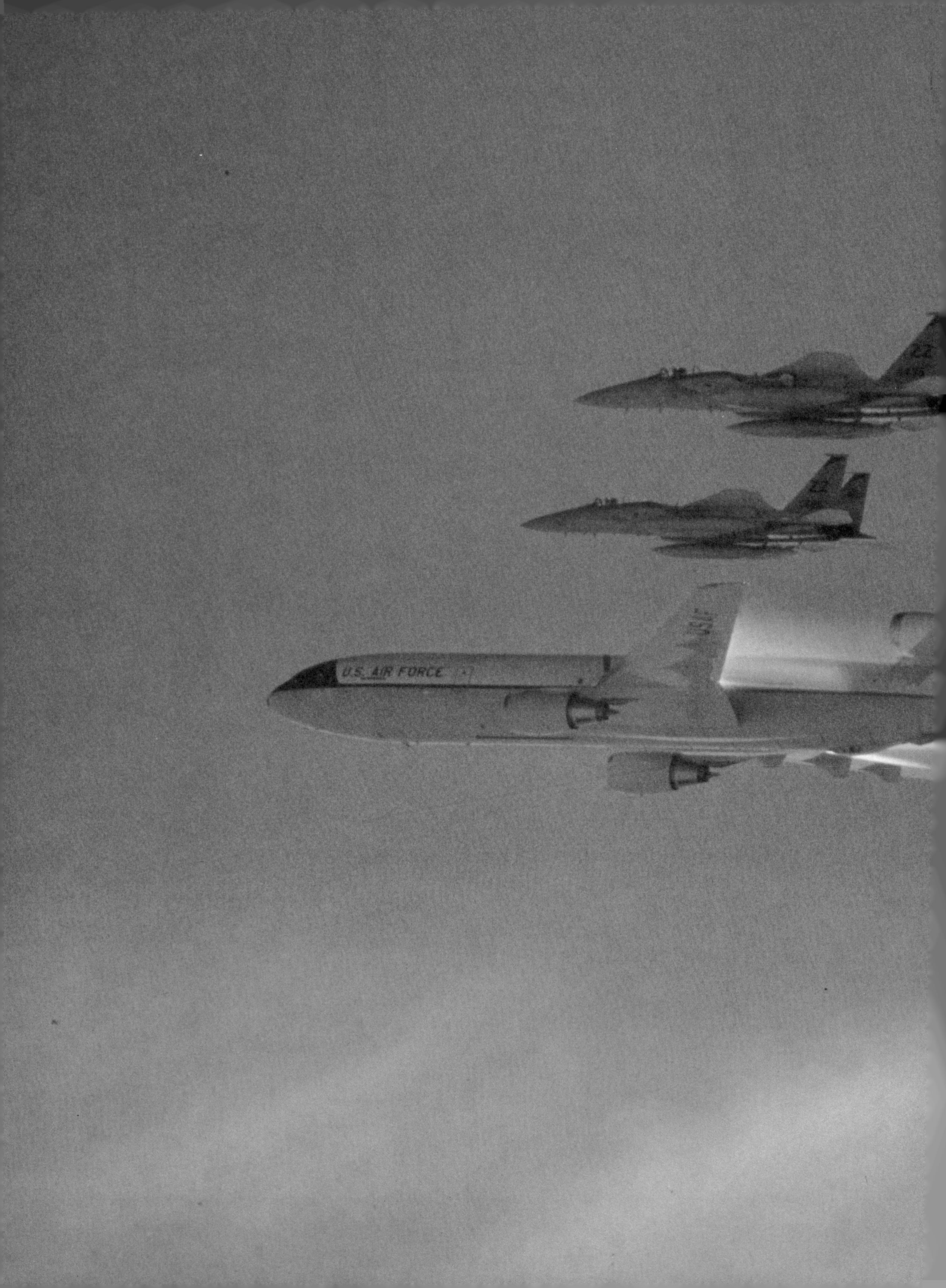
U.S. AIR FORCE

It is said that the F-15 Eagle is the top of the line; what all the young guys going to pilot training dream about. And should they ultimately get checked out in that F-15, most hope they are on their way to Europe afterwards. After all, everyone knows that if things ever get really get "hot" it will be here. The American F-15 pilots are thoroughly trained and extremely proud of their machines. The training is so intense and the standards are so high, that to have earned operational status in an F-15 in USAFE is something one can be really proud of.

The USA's involvement in Europe goes back to WWII when US fighters and bombers, flying from bases principally in Britain, joined the fight against Nazi Germany. When the war ended, some remained to help "clean up", but in June 1948 the Soviets blockaded Berlin and the Americans staged their famous Berlin Airlift. Over 150,000 flights were made in order to bring supplies into the isolated city. In 1949, NATO was formed and the United States, its strongest member, operated a number of bases in Europe.

Today, the F-15 is one of USAFE's strongest weapons in Europe. To optimize their wartime capabilities, they are stationed as close as possible to the border between East and West Germany. In daily exercises with other NATO countries, the Eagles have earned a reputation as formidable adversaries and the F-15 pilots proudly display their "Eagle Drivers" patches. The American F-15 pilots in Europe modestly deny they are the world's best fighter pilots, but they fight hard for that same reputation in their daily training missions which span from Iceland to Turkey and from West Germany to Gibraltar.

There is a queue at the airborne gas station 30,000 feet over the North Pacific. The tanker, a KC-10 is a welcome sight for the thirsty F-15s on their way from Japan to Alaska.

... JUST AN ORDINARY DAY!

July 4th, 1989, 250 million Americans celebrating their country's birthday – but there isn't much celebrating for two F-15 pilots on an air base in West Germany. They are on "Zulu Alert" – a 24-hour guard over the border between East and West Germany. On the other side of the Iron Curtain, two of their Warsaw Pact counterparts are doing the same thing.

Both pilots received a set of classified authenticators before stepping to their jets. It is only through proper use of these authenticators that they can be scrambled. On July 4th, the proper codes were passed and three minutes later the F-15s raced into the sky on what would prove to be an amazing mission.

The two Eagles had no idea what was in store as they sped eastward. They contacted GCI (ground controlled intercept) on a discrete frequency and received the course and altitude of an unidentified fighter which had not responded to radio calls, didn't have a flight plan, and was continuing westward over the border into West Germany. Ten minutes later the Eagles intercepted the unknown fighter, which turned out to be a Soviet MiG-23. The first F-15 closed on the MiG for a closer look as the second remained in trail with his finger on the trigger. Seconds later came the shocking discovery which was immediately passed to GCI: "The Russian fighter doesn't have a pilot!"

The response came a moment later to the two astonished Eagle-drivers: "We don't know what's going on, but if it threatens a populated area, shoot it down." Eagle 1: "It could be carrying atomic weapons. It's impossible for us to see." The Eagles followed the pilotless MiG for 300 miles while other F-15s prepared to relieve them along the course the MiG appeared to be holding. This alarming flight continued over West Germany, Holland, and Belgium as it headed for the English Channel. The responsibility of shooting down the MiG rested entirely with the Eagle flight lead. Shooting down the fighter over a city could have catastrophic results, unimaginable in magnitude if it was carrying atomic weapons. Seconds ticked by as everyone waited for an explanation from the Soviet Union – still nothing.

After following it for 500 miles, the two F-15 pilots watched helplessly as the MiG's engine flamed out. The jet crashed into a house in the small Belgian town of Kooigem killing a 19-year-old boy. A few minutes more and it would have smashed into the large French city of Lille.

Later it was explained that the MiG-23's pilot, a highly decorated colonel, had ejected shortly after takeoff thinking the jet was about to explode. Instead, it continued on autopilot for nearly 600 miles.

This episode could have had awful consequences and has led to a great deal of discussion between NATO and the Warsaw Pact nations concerning the lack of a timely explanation for the MiG. Both sides have agreed, to the great relief of their alert pilots, to establish a "Hot Line", in an attempt to prevent incidents like this in the future.

For the two American fighter pilots, it was just another day far from home...

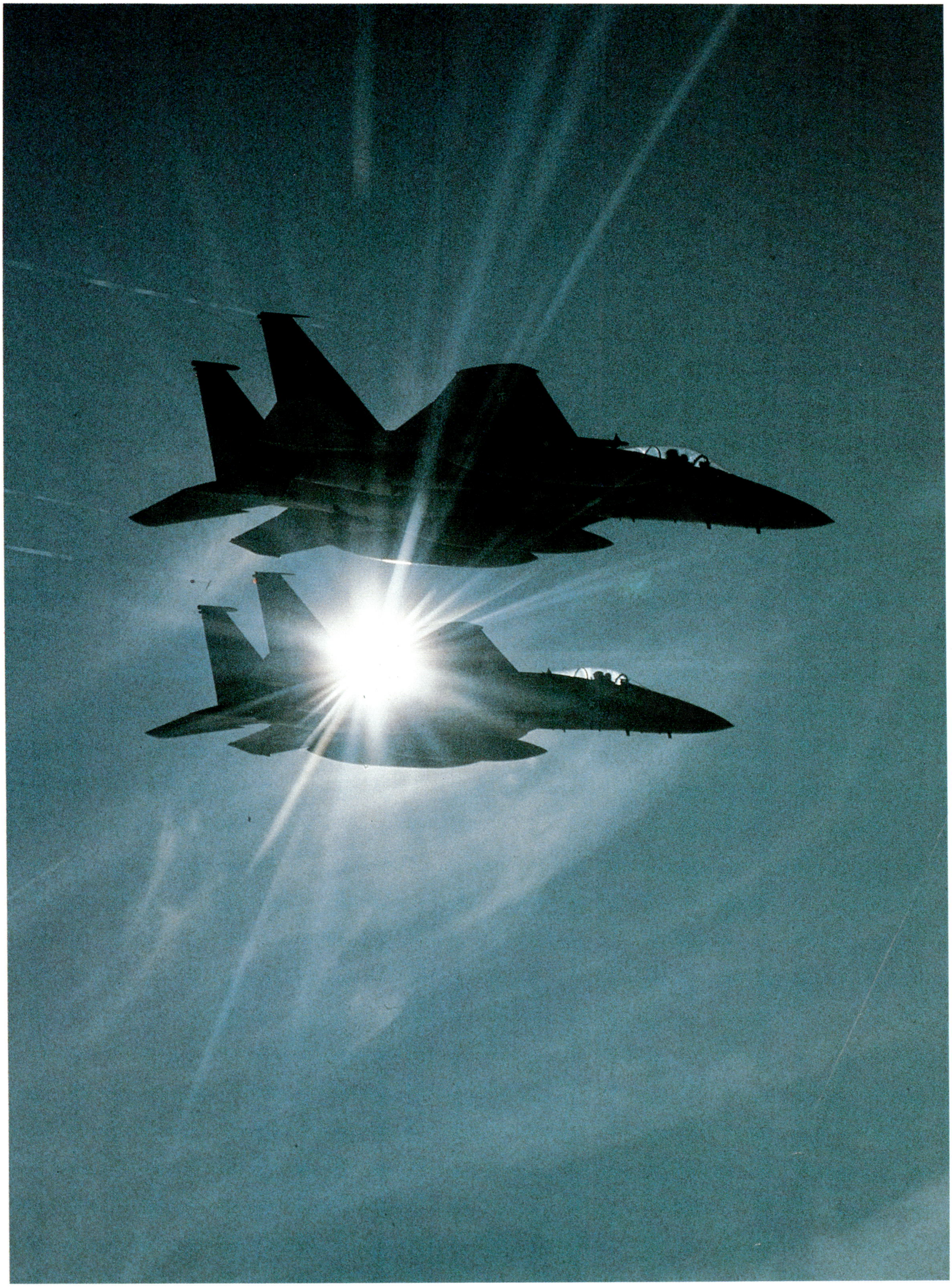

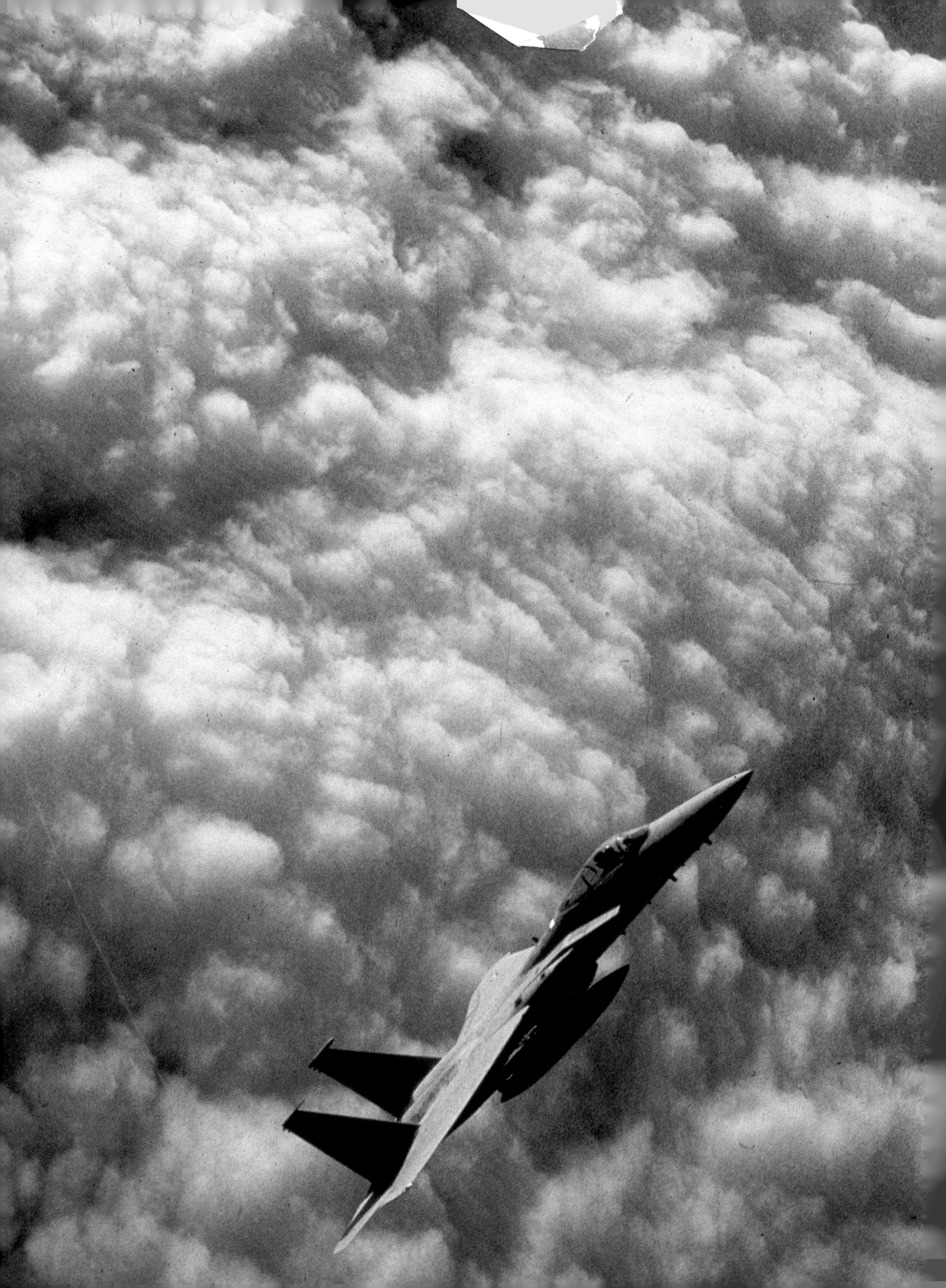

**Close to merging with the gloomy clouds somewhere over Europe, an Eagle-driver from Bitburg, West Germany, feels pretty alone up there on his Zulu Alert.
But up where he belongs — at 50,000 feet — the sky is always blue — and a beautiful world for the few who make their living up there.**

"The F-16 Fighting Falcon is the perfect machine for a dogfight. With its HUD (Heads-Up-Display) and "hands-on" dogfight override avionics, the pilot's toughest job is sometimes just withstanding the 9 Gs, which the F-16 is capable of. Under this much G force you can barely lift a hand. Fortunately, the jet's sidestick controller and fly-by-wire flight controls make flying the airplane a little easier than a conventional fighter under similar conditions. GLOC (G-induced Loss Of Consciousness) is a very real threat in the F-16 and we make every attempt to build up our tolerance against it by training in a high G environment every day. Some pilots naturally have higher G-tolerances than others, but one thing is certain: only those in top shape can truly play the game.

It is safe to say the F-16 has done an outstanding job fulfilling its task as a multirole fighter for USAFE (US Air Forces in Europe). Together with our NATO allies, of which many also fly the F-16, we have put together a strong team. The F-16's primary role is that of a 'mud-beater', going in low and fast in an attempt to stay under radar cover and hold enemy fighters at a distance until the designated target has been taken out.

"You can call us a fast fist in the air, where big brother F-15 handles the heavy stuff. The F-15 mission is to establish a chain of defense by keeping enemy bombers away from our territory. They do their part effectively, mostly because of their sophisticated radar systems. So they keep their part of the sky clean – we keep ours!"

F-16 pilot, USAFE

Above: An F-16 pilot can be a very lonely man – especially in clouds like this and keeping total radio silence.

RS stands for Ramstein, where US Air Forces Europe has close to 100 F-16s. Overleaf: formation of F-16s from USAFE's Hahn AB, West Germany.

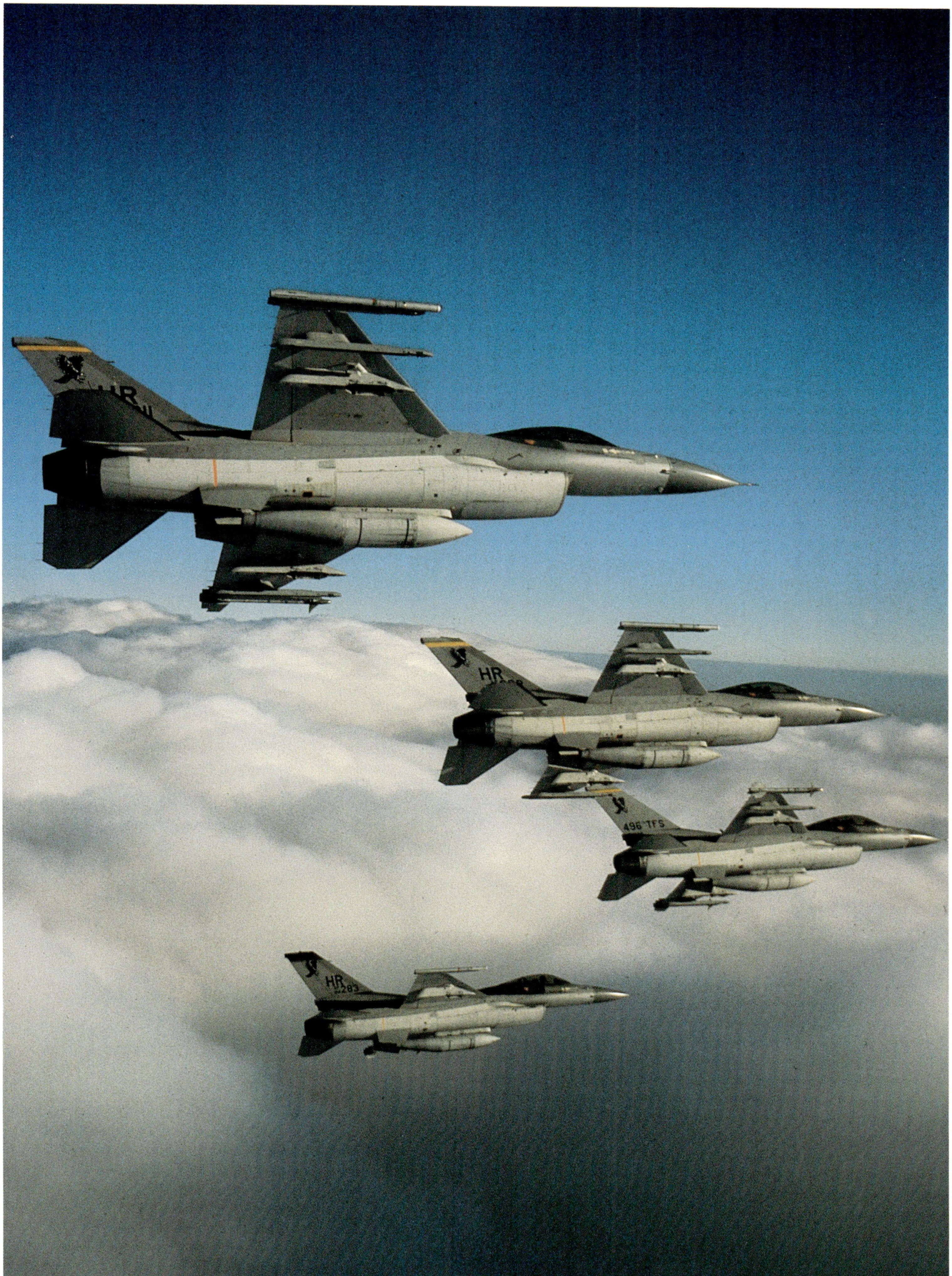
HR
496 TFS
HR

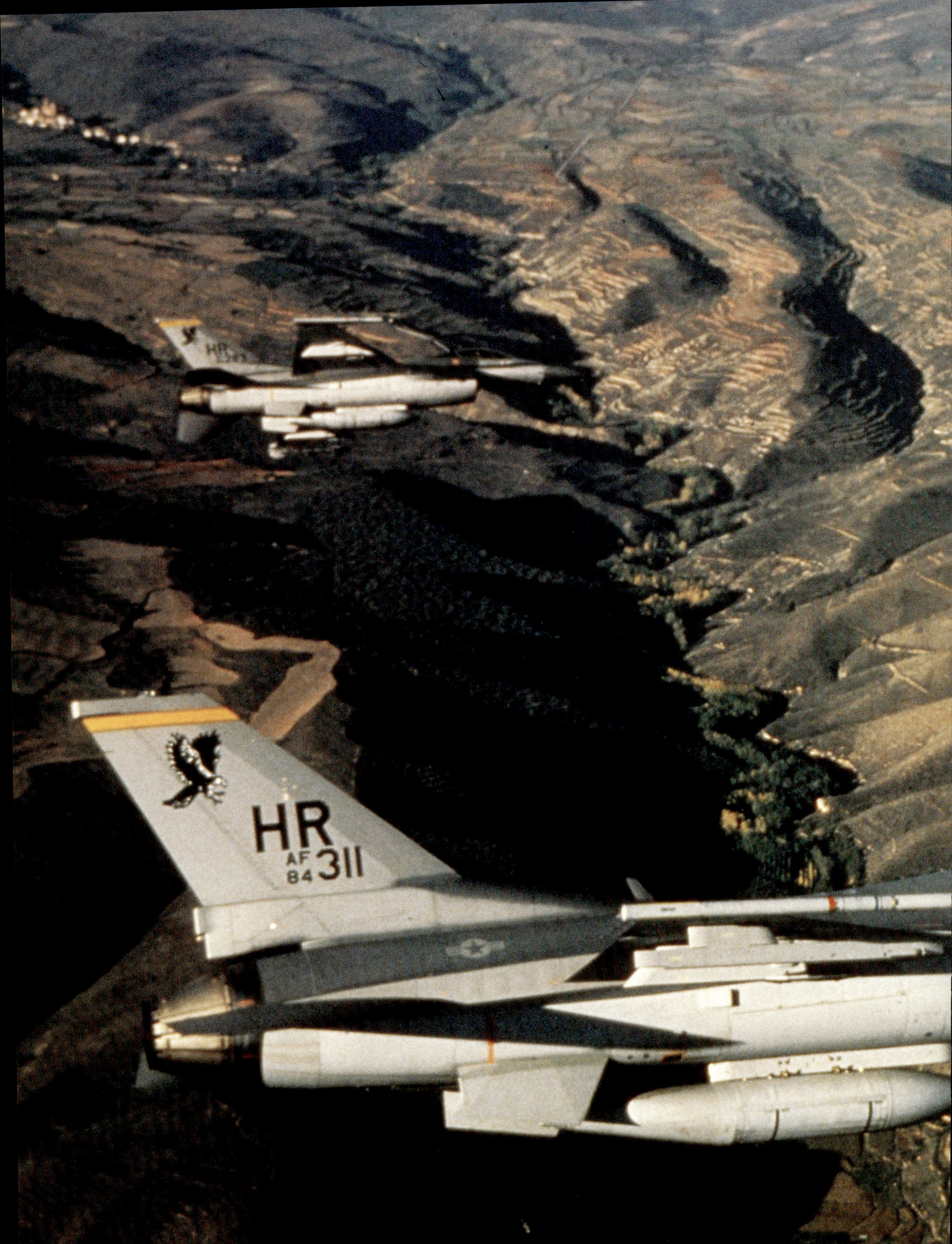
HR
AF
84 311

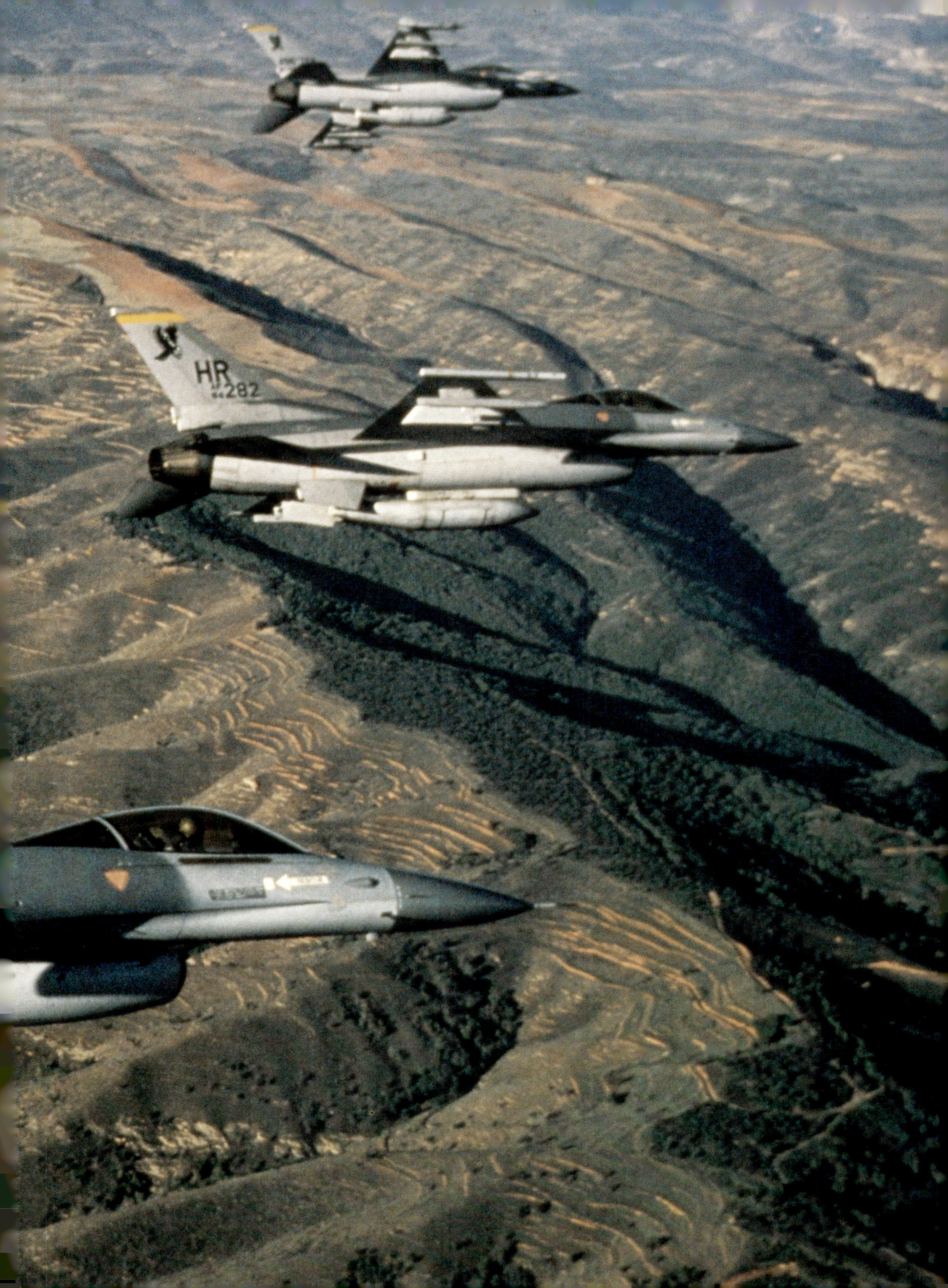
HR
282

" The speed is 9 miles/minute! As you race just above the surface of the earth, trees race by on both sides of the cockpit, and mountains tower in front of you. The jet rolls onto its side and for a moment you think your wingtip will strike the ground. You feel as if you've been shot over the earth by some unbelievable power. Your pulse thunders and every nerve ending is excited. It is speed like you've never dreamed of. It is invigorating and it is uncomfortable at the same time. You are scared of it, but you still get wild enjoyment from it.

"When I was learning to fly the F-111, I was quickly overwhelmed by the sensation of supersonic, low altitude flying. My instructor would tap the map on his kneeboard and say: 'Look at this, look at your instruments, look at anything, but don't look out the window!' Fortunately, there's no real need to look out the window. Everything you need to know is on your instrument panel. I have to admit though, seeing 200 feet on the altimeter and Mach 1 on the airspeed indicator doesn't get you quite as worked up as seeing trees race by your wingtips and mountains looming in front of you as the terrain-following radar picks your way through them.

"I am on my third year hear at Lakenheath, England where the 48th Tactical Fighter Wing is stationed. I was a combat ready fighter jock at Nellis Air Force Base in Nevada when I was chosen for the F-111 program. The F-111 check out took one year and it was another year in the squadron after that before I was fully operational. We lose a lot of people during the initial F-111 training, some people just can't handle it. We actually prefer night and bad weather where we can fully take advantage of our TFR system. The F-111 pioneered the TFR (Terrain Following Radar), an integrated ground radar and autopilot which can guide the jet just 50 feet over the terrain at supersonic speeds. We can fly regardless of the weather, hell, we fly in anything. With aerial refuelling, we can deliver our 15 ton payload anywhere in Europe.

"It was the F-111 that shut Gadhaffi's mouth a few years back. We were so heavily loaded when we bombed Tripoli, we had to refuel eight nerve-wracking times during the 14 hour mission. We obviously only meant to teach him a lesson because we could have hit him a lot harder than we did with our laser-guided bombs. The laser-guided weapons are operated by the WSO, the weapons system officer sitting next to the pilot, who finds the target with the laser which guides the weapons to meet it. The system is close to 100% effective.

"The F-111 is a bomber, but it isn't quite as vulnerable to fighters as most bombers. We have the speed and endurance to slip away from them. We can hold Mach 2.2 at 50,000 feet longer than most fighters. If everything goes wrong it isn't an ejection seat that will save us, but a capsule. The whole cockpit is more or less a kind of space capsule, which is jettisoned free from the jet by a rocket motor. After 'ejection', the pilot and WSO float to earth together under the same parachute.

"In an F-111, you simply have to trust your instruments and forget everything going on outside your window. The airplane's TFR is the be all and end all here. You can also forget the stories about the first F-111s of which three were lost during the first month they flew in Vietnam. They were called back, analyzed, their problems were corrected, and they were sent back to the front. Only during the first missions were jets lost, primarily due to a fault in the TFR.

"Because of this, the F-111 earned a bad reputation and pilots didn't exactly stand in line to gamble their lives on a radar. Things have changed since then. If you were born with speed in your blood, the cure is the F-111... "

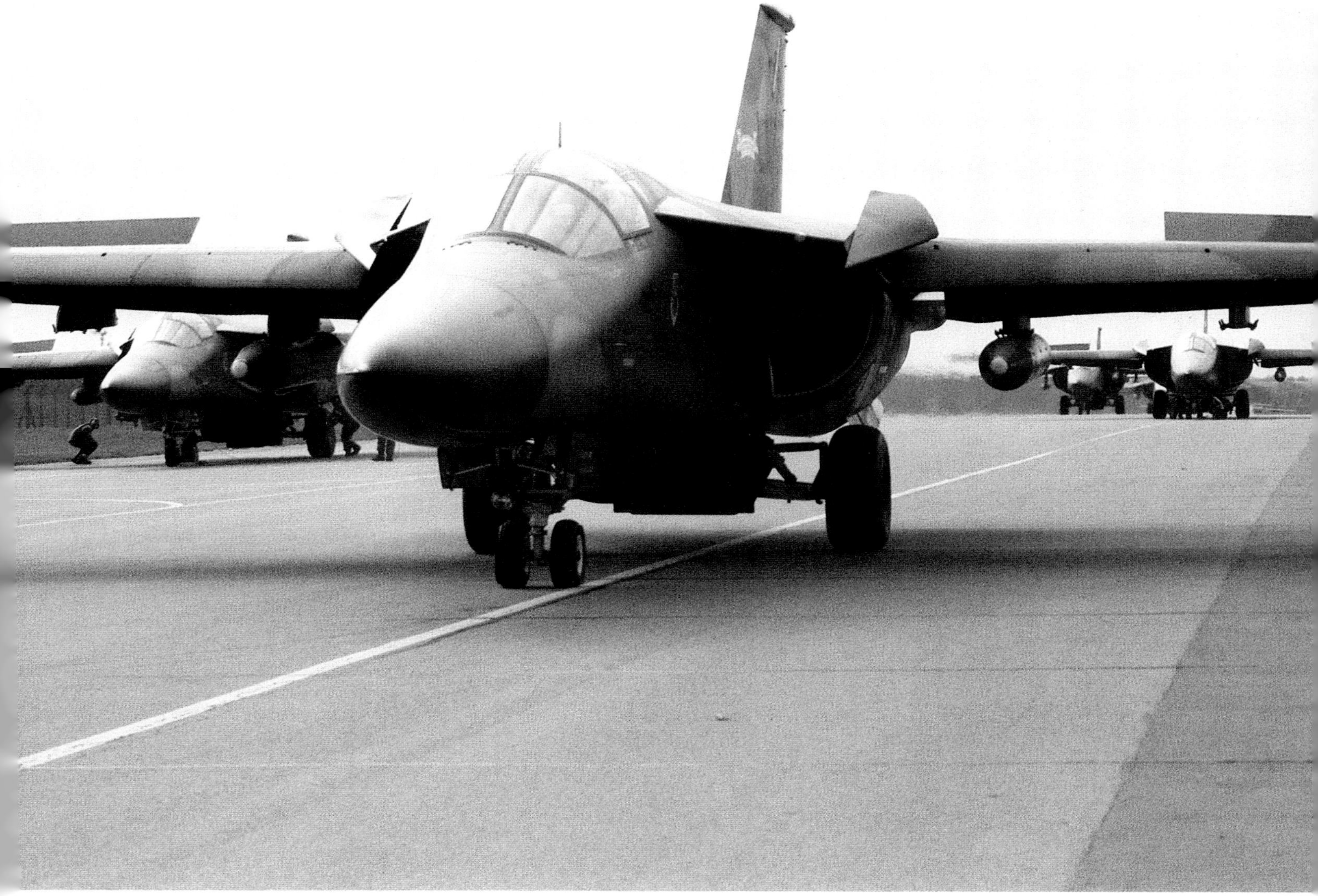

LN — Lakenheath, England. Home of the 48th Tactical Fighter Wing — and that means F-111! Here one of the one-elevens is approaching an airtanker over the North Sea, but this job will never be routine — and while the pilot concentrates on his instruments, his radar system officer keeps an eye on the coupling.

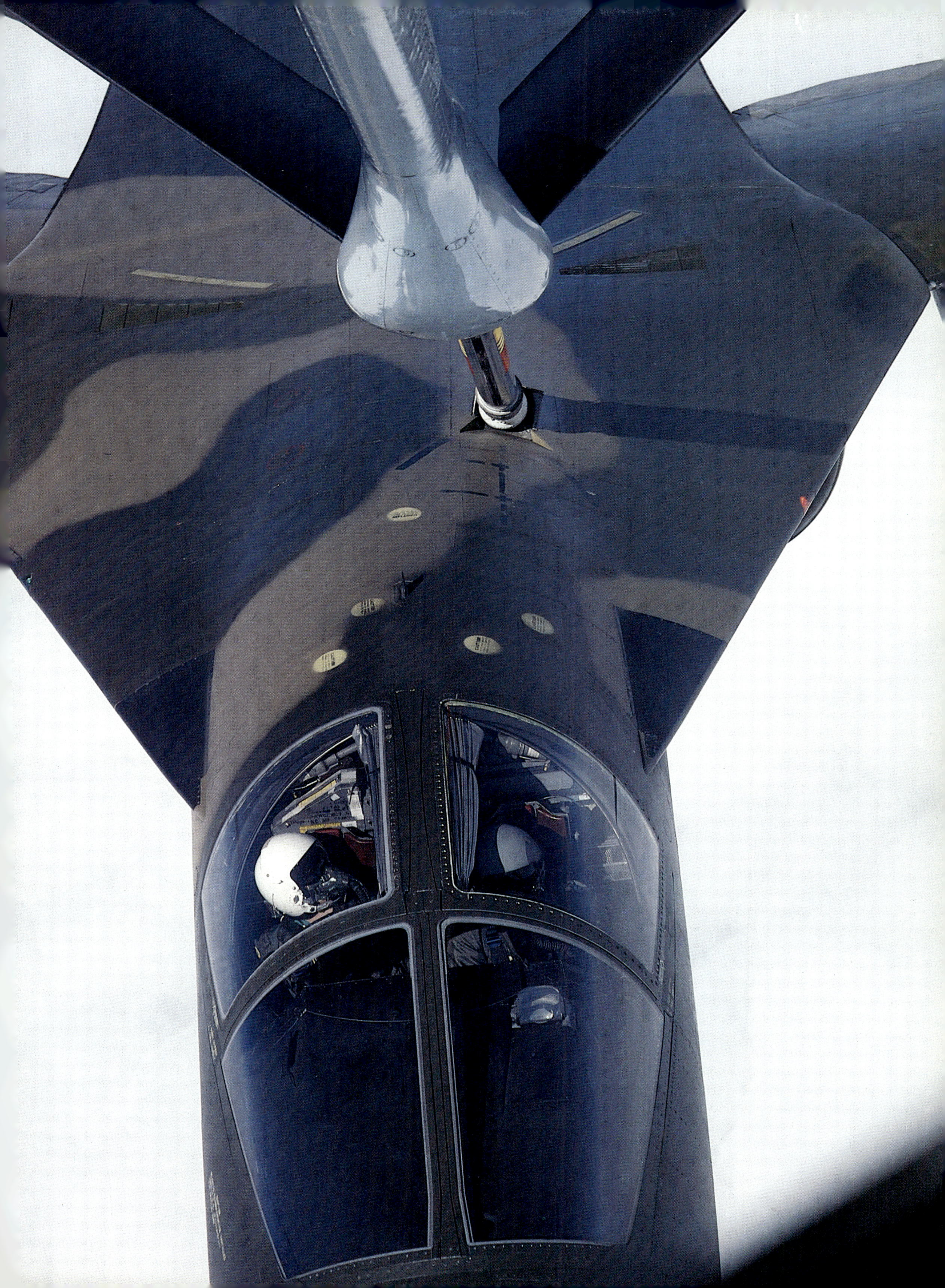

The B-1B bomber is a member of the USA's alert force and a regular guest in the European skies. As a watchdog, the heavy bomber will often be waiting over the North Pole for 20 hours, ready to reach Moscow in 30 minutes if necessary. Aerial refuelling will normally take place over Greenland or Scandinavia. It is a lonely and boring job for the four crew members. Hour after hour on the other side of the clouds, waiting for a radio call nobody ever wants to hear.

The crew are always veterans. The pilots – a captain and a co-pilot, have years of experience from the FB-111, a brother in the bomber-family.

In the back seat of the bomber a defence officer and a younger attack officer work. Together, the four men control the most advanced super-bomber in the world. And with them rides the awareness that the B-1Bs have suffered some unexplained and fatal crashes.

Maybe the future lies with missiles and space weapons, but the country that invented flying machines still believes in the human factor. The Americans don't want dangerous weapons controlled from underground bunkers. They want men up there, men who understand the responsibility. 400 of them fly the 100 B-1B bombers of the US Air Force...

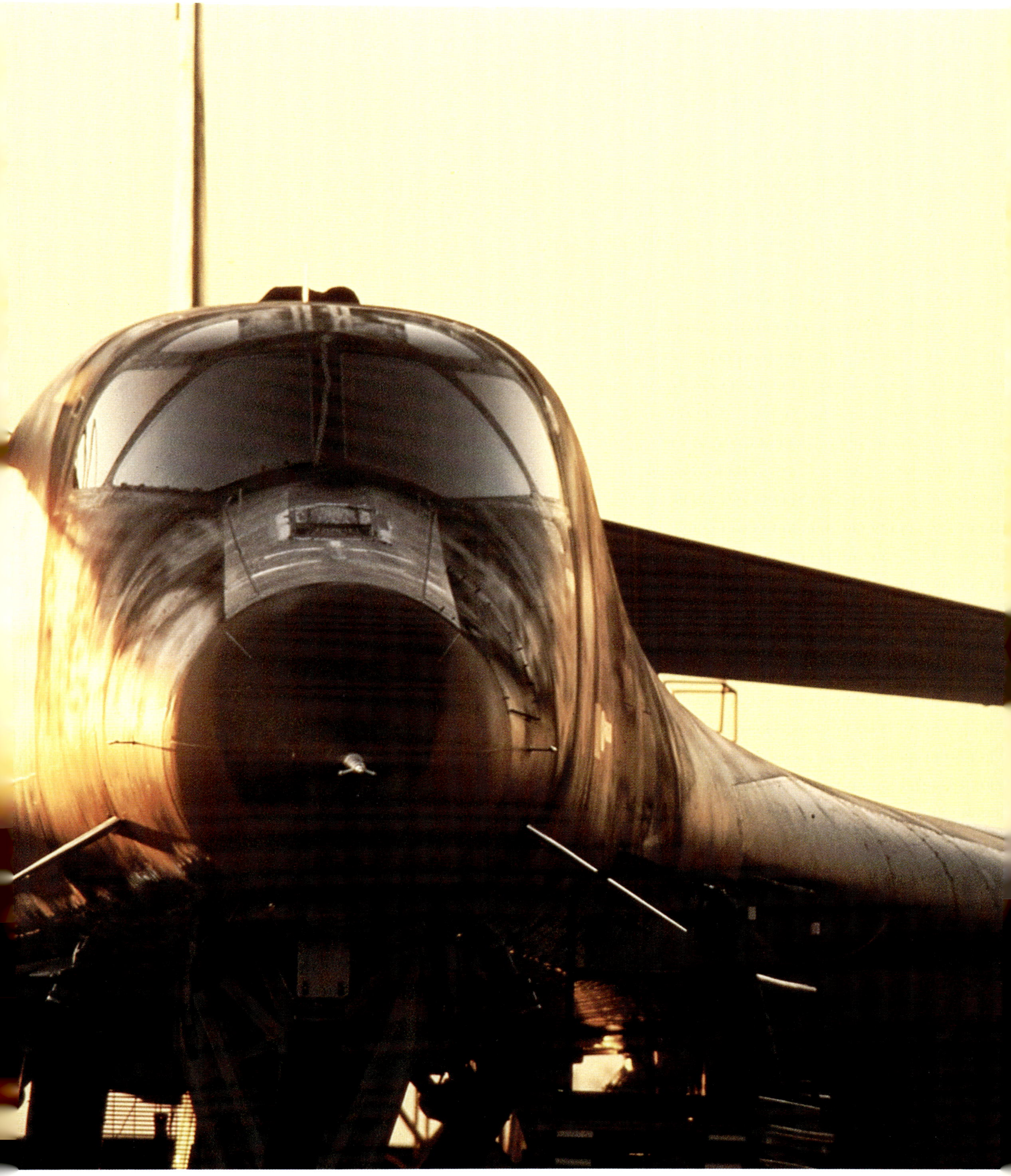

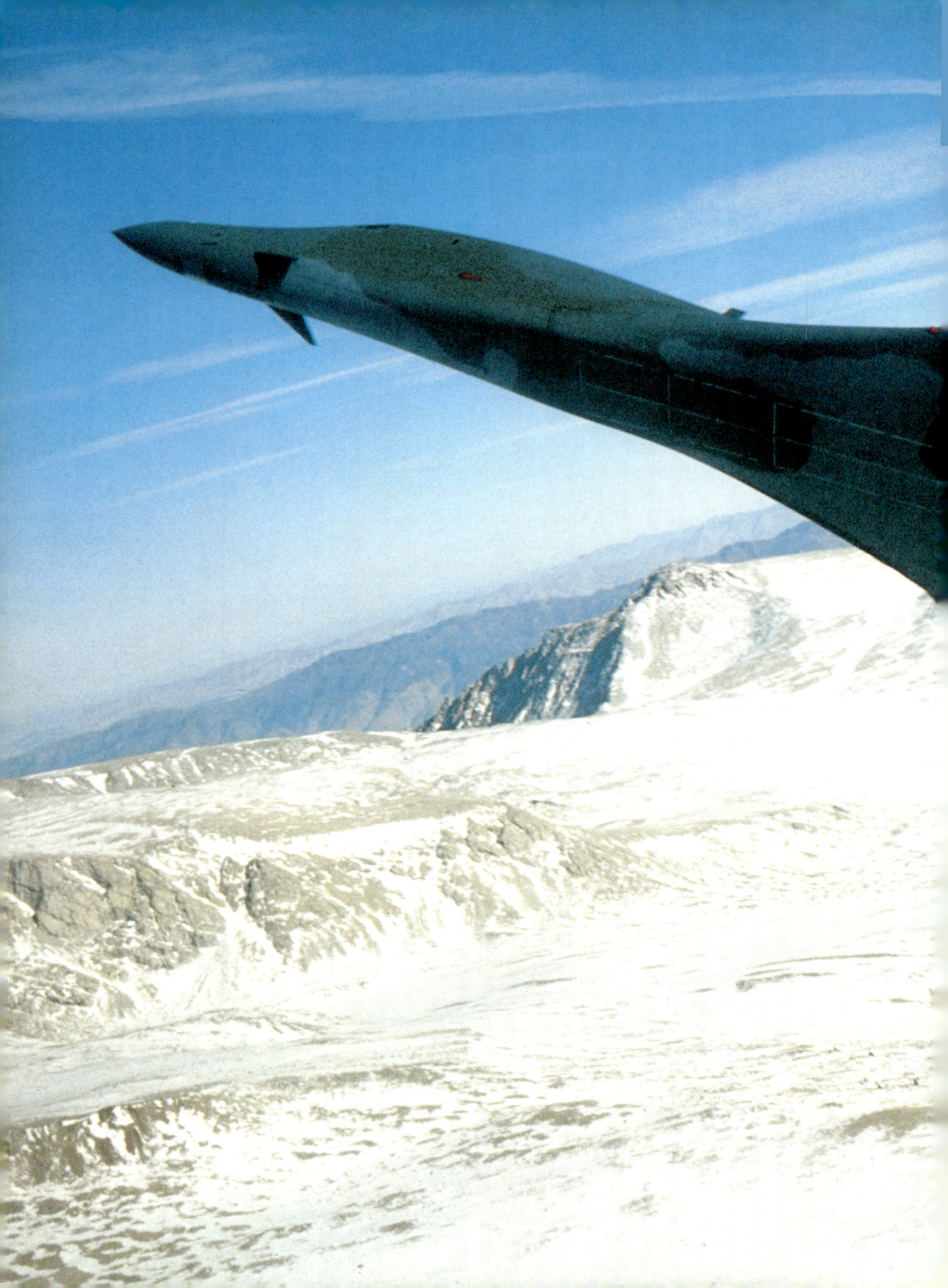

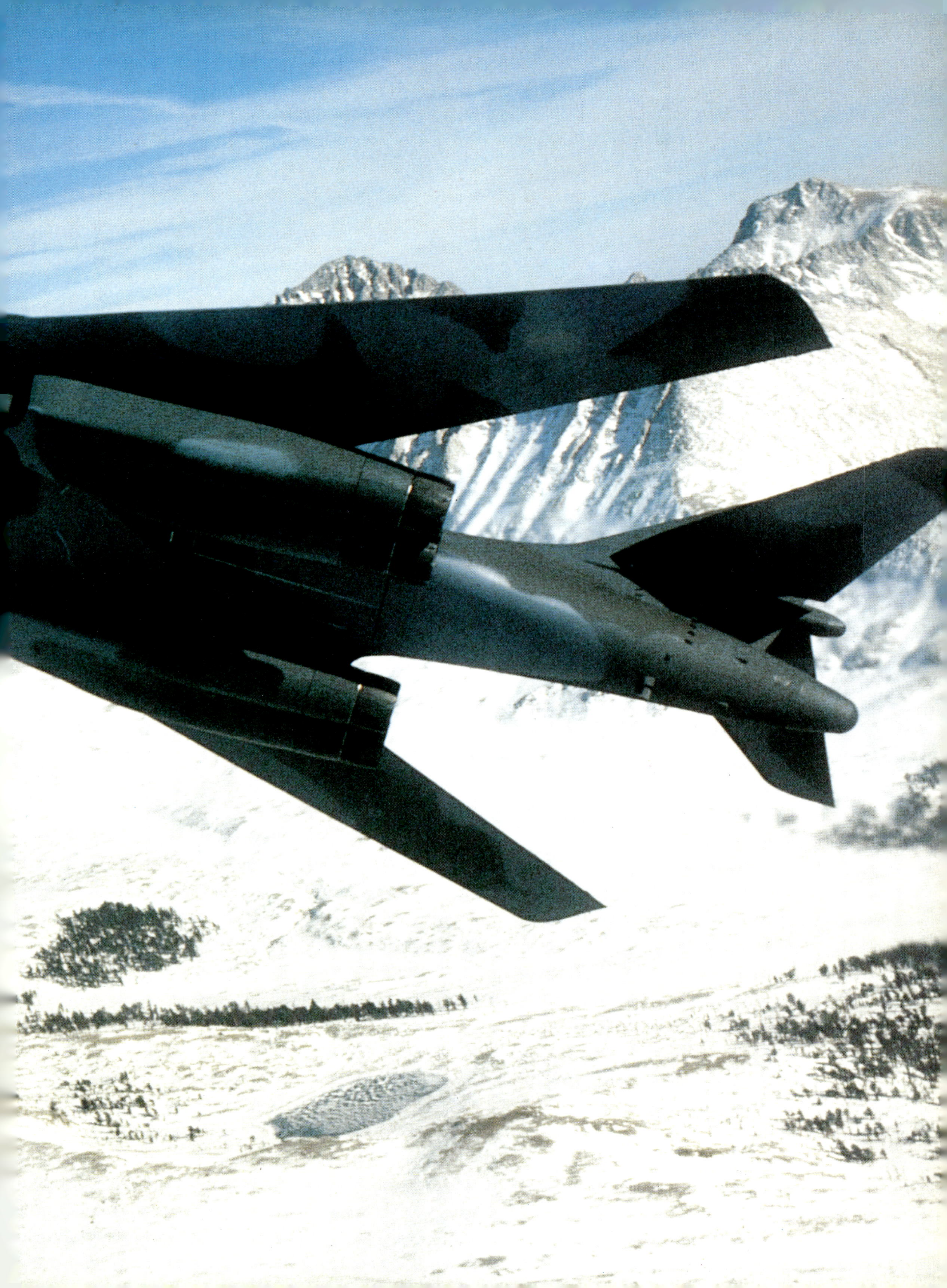

BYE BYE BLACKBIRD

"My Blackbird is twenty years old and it is still years ahead of its time.

"They call it an airplane. Well, okay, I guess an SR-71 is an airplane in about the same way an atomic submarine is a boat!

"We that fly the Lockheed SR-71 operate more in space than we do in the sky. It is dark at 80,000 feet. For some that is exhilarating, for others it is uncomfortable. We are intensively trained in altitude psychology, but most of us have been scared at some point in time. You feel you are just too far out in space! 'What goes up must come down' is how the old saying goes. Well, it feels as if that might not necessarily apply out there. Your altimeter and your altitude indicator are the only things you can really trust.

"There are two men on board the world's fastest and highest flying airplane. A pilot and the electronic systems officer. We wear specially designed pressure suits when flying the SR-71 and we don't fly a mission that we haven't planned for hours in advance. Although they're somewhat cumbersome we can't fly without our pressure suits – at that altitude our blood would boil. We also undergo intensive yearly physicals and are examined by a specialist before every mission. When you fly the SR-71 you have to face the fact that it is a lifestyle. You can no longer live like ordinary people. You must work to maintain your own body in the same working order as your jet.

"We are constantly looking for possible candidates for the Blackbird as we always run the risk that one of our aircrew will be grounded. This can happen even if he has maintained the fitness standard expected of Air Force pilots.

"It can be tough spending 10 hours in a spacesuit. I have had missions where I had to be helped from the cockpit. Our home base is Beale AFB in California, but our areas of operation make it necessary for us to operate from bases all over the world. We are often in England and northern Norway, which is no secret because we don't and can't carry any weapons on the SR-71. Many people feel the SR-71 is the embodiment of death and destruction; quite the opposite. We may be one of the most advanced airplanes with a top speed of Mach 3 (approx. 1800 knots) and an operational altitude over 80,000 feet, but we are also one of the most peaceful. We fly for the Strategic Air Command's 9th Strategic Reconnaissance Wing and our most important mission is to keep an eye on what's going on below with the help of our advanced cameras. We can cover 120,000 square miles in 1 hour at 80,000 feet.

"The SR-71 cannot be compared with any other airplane. It must be able to withstand extreme structural changes due to the tremendous range of environments it operates in. Since it was designed to spend most of its time at tremendous altitude, it doesn't function quite so well on the ground. The special titanium skin was constructed to allow for the expansion of the metal which occurs at the high temperatures associated with flight at Mach 3. The net result is that it leaks like a sieve on the ground where the metal has not yet expanded. We also use a tremendous amount of fuel during takeoff as the engines are very inefficient at low altitude. Because of this, we usually go directly to a tanker after takeoff. SR-71 missions are always covered by a net of tankers that wait for us in special air corridors. It takes many hundreds of support personnel to accomplish every single Blackbird mission.

"I am proud of my plane, although I feel more like an astronaut than I do a pilot. When we fly supersonically the jet is always on autopilot because it is not humanly possible to fly steadily enough for the cameras. At subsonic speeds we hand fly the airplane and she handles like a dream. If you appreciate extreme altitudes, speeds and claustrophobic surroundings rather than fear them, there isn't a better jet to fly than the SR-71."

A Blackbird pilot

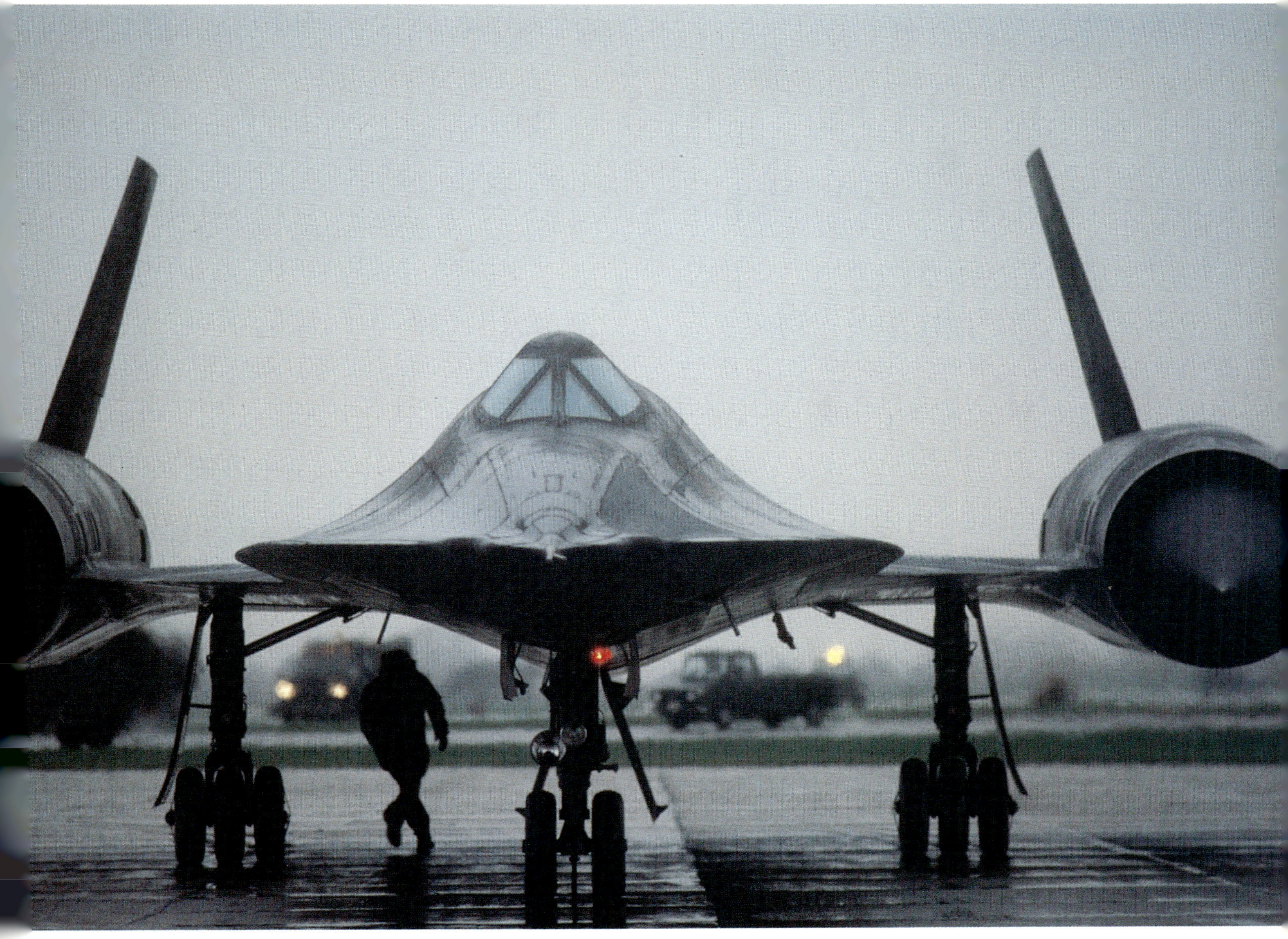

"Okay, we know, we're ugly and the chances are pretty slim that the Nimrod will be the star of the next *Top Gun* film. Our world is just not very romantic. We have the difficult task of finding and waging war on submarines, ships or anything which tries to take control of the seas. We are a flying computer which, through the use of sophisticated sensors, can instantly identify a ship we haven't even seen yet. This aside, it's a tough job to be the sheriff of a large ocean. We cruise along at 30,000 feet and 400 knots searching for possible targets. If needed, we can descend to just over the ocean's surface and shut down two engines to save fuel. Here we can literally sniff out the exhaust of the submarines.

"It is a dramatic sight to see this large jet airplane whip over the ocean at 420 knots. We often have missions lasting up to 20 hours; they are both physically and mentally demanding. Night or day doesn't matter to us. We have spotlights which throw out 70 million candle power. We are primarily a bomber/inspection airplane, but we can serve in many roles, as we proved during the Falkland War.

"The Nimrod's history began as a commercial airliner known as the Comet. The Comet, however, didn't have the same succes as the military version. The Royal Air Force operates approximately 50 of these four-engine jets, which have such an important mission, especially over the North Atlantic. Nimrods operate from RAF Kinloss in Scotland and RAF St. Mawgan in Southwest England.

Nimrod-pilot, RAF

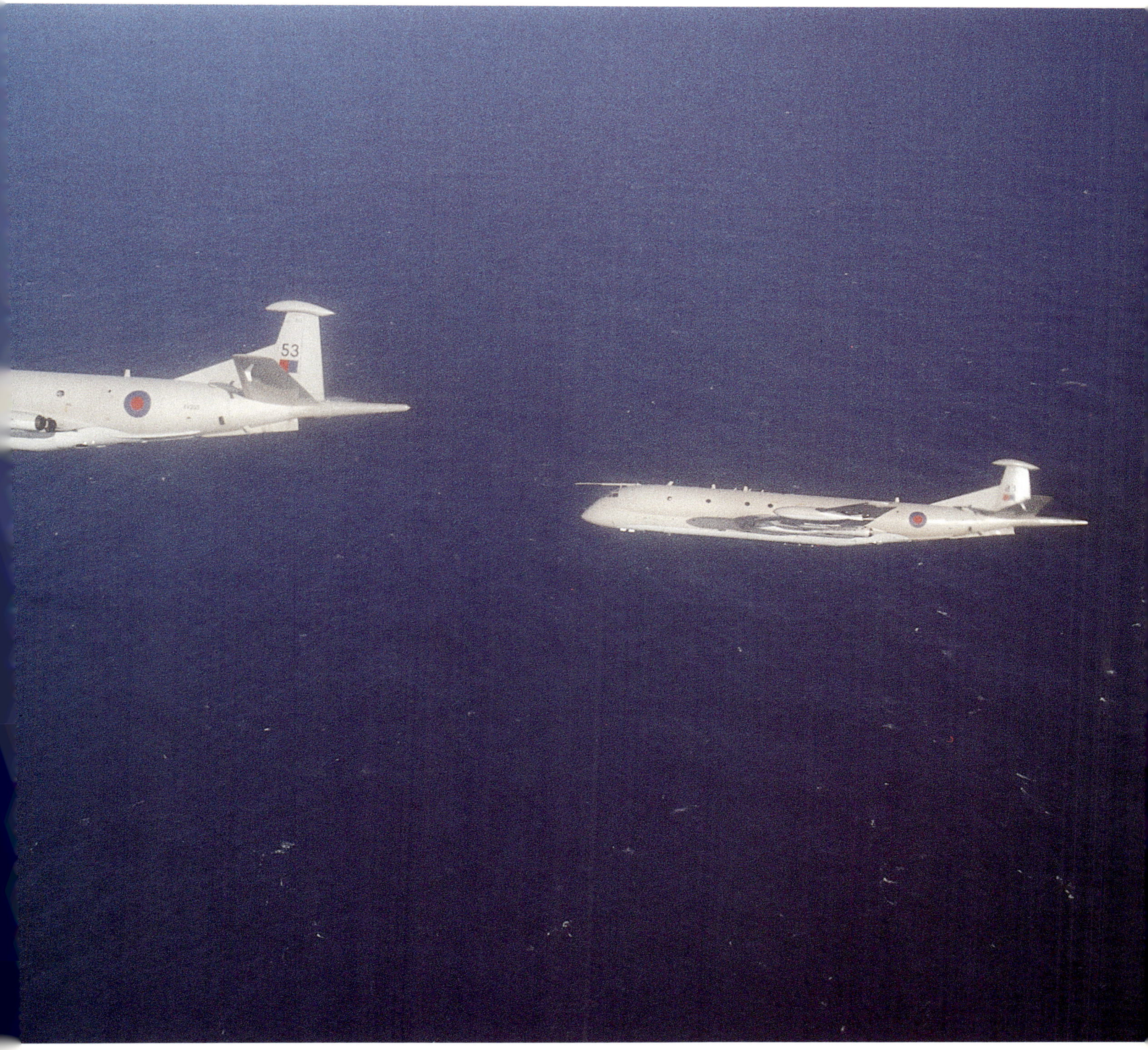
53

THE EYE IN THE SKY

– We are 18 people on board from eight different nations: The captain is from Turkey, the co-pilot from West Germany, the navigator from Holland, and the radar technician from Denmark. Naturally, we have just one way of communication – English. Fortunately, that is also the language in which we were trained to operate our $150 million AWACS (airborne warning and control system).

In most respects, the AWACS looks like an ordinary airliner, which is not surprising because the airframe is that of a Boeing 707. In its military configuration, it is known as the E-3A and is one of the world's most expensive airplanes. In fact, the E3-A is an airborne surveillance and warning platform which, under the NATO flag, watches over a large portion of the world between the Arctic Ocean in the north and the Mediterranean in the south. The disklike rotating rotodome 15 feet over the lead-lined aircraft skin beneath it (this is to guard against the radiation emitted by the rotodome) covers a powerful radar that is capable of scanning the area for hundreds of miles with amazing resolution. From 30,000 feet over the North Sea near the Norwegian island of Spitsbergen, the E3-A can detect a fighter which has just taken off from a Russian base. If necessary, it can scramble a pair of Norwegian fighters to intercept it long before the inbound fighter becomes a threat.

The AWACS is an indispensible part of NATO's defense network. The US designed airplane operates with an international crew compiled from most of the member nations. The AWACS mission is so crucial that only the most qualified personnel are accepted. A co-pilot must have at least 1200 hours on multi-engine jets, a captain at least 2000. The flight crew consists of four people, while 14 are required to service the radar and communications equipment. An AWACS can remain airborne for 11 hours at a time without aerial refuelling, but a mission may last as long as 18 hours. Fortunately, the missions are routine in that the radar detects nothing out of the ordinary. Unfortunately, this means many long and boring hours in the sky. To maintain their fighting edge, AWACS participate nearly every day in various NATO exercises being conducted all over the world. In Europe alone, their are at least two which between them provide 24-hour surveillance.

Officially, NATO's 18 Boeing E3-As are based in Luxembourg, but in reality their main operating base is Geilenkirchen in West Germany. The big, powerful plane is frequently seen on many major bases throughout NATO and specially trained technicians are permanently stationed at bases in Norway, Turkey, Italy, and Greece. NATO/OTAN (OTAN is french for NATO) E3-As look exactly like the American version, but the advanced technology which put the airplane into the $150 million dollar class is mostly of European origin. AWACS is unarmed, although it could carry air-to-air missiles for self defense. Even with these air-to-air missiles, it would prove an easy target for enemy fighters. Because of this, the AWACS would be heavily protected by NATO fighters in time of war.

– E-3A pilot

MODERN DAY VIKINGS

It is through these waters Erik the Red sailed 1000 years ago on his way to Greenland where he was the first Viking to set foot on the largest of the world's islands. His son, Leif the Cheerful, sailed the same route on his way to discovering North America – 500 years before Colombus.

1000 years have passed and very little has changed. The weather and waters of the North Atlantic are just as harsh. Today, fishermen from all over the world have come to the North Atlantic to earn their livings. To do so in this treacherous corner of the world has led to countless accidents and incidents requiring emergency assistance.

Enter the "Modern Day Vikings"!

In Danish they're know as the Søflyverne, a small corps of specially trained helicopter pilots. Flying the blue Lynx helicopter, they have saved countless lives in the last 25 years they have operated in the North Atlantic. The brave Lynx pilots are faced with a demanding existence, spending three months at a time aboard a Danish inspection ship. It is from the small helicopter platform in the stern of the inspection ships that the Danish Navy's rescue helicopters operate.

Their mission is first and foremost to rescue people in distress, but they also represent Danish sovereignty in Greenland and the Faroe Islands. The rescue pilots are continually faced with the worst imaginable weather and many times are faced with choosing between following procedures to the letter of the law or looking the other way long enough to hoist that last sailor from his stranded trawler knowing that with every passing minute the weather will get worse and his sole landing place on the stern of the inspection ship will be more difficult to find. This, however, is something that isn't discussed by these modern day Vikings – it's just done.

The Danish Lynx pilots stand out year after year at the basic helicopter training course at Fort Rucker, Alabama, USA, where they consistently earn top scores. In fact, the Danish pilots average 98% where the overall average is 88%.

They expect nothing less from themselves as they strive to live up to the proud traditions of the waters which they serve.

On the following page, a Lynx helicopter waits for take-off clearance on the stern of the Danish Navy inspection ship INGOLF. There are four men aboard the Lynx: the pilot, who sits in the right seat, and his systems operator in the left. In the back, a doctor and a paramedic who operate the helicopter's rescue hoist.

This is how the world looks to a Viking of the 1990s: Lynx helicopters operate all over the rough seas of the North Atlantic where temperatures often reach –30°C. During prolonged rescue missions, the helicopter's sliding door is constantly open, forcing the pilot to operate his helicopter's intricate switches with heavily gloved hands. It can also be beautiful up in the North Atlantic – as the Lynx helicopters return to their ships with a background of the same icebergs which Eric the Red may have seen 1000 years ago.

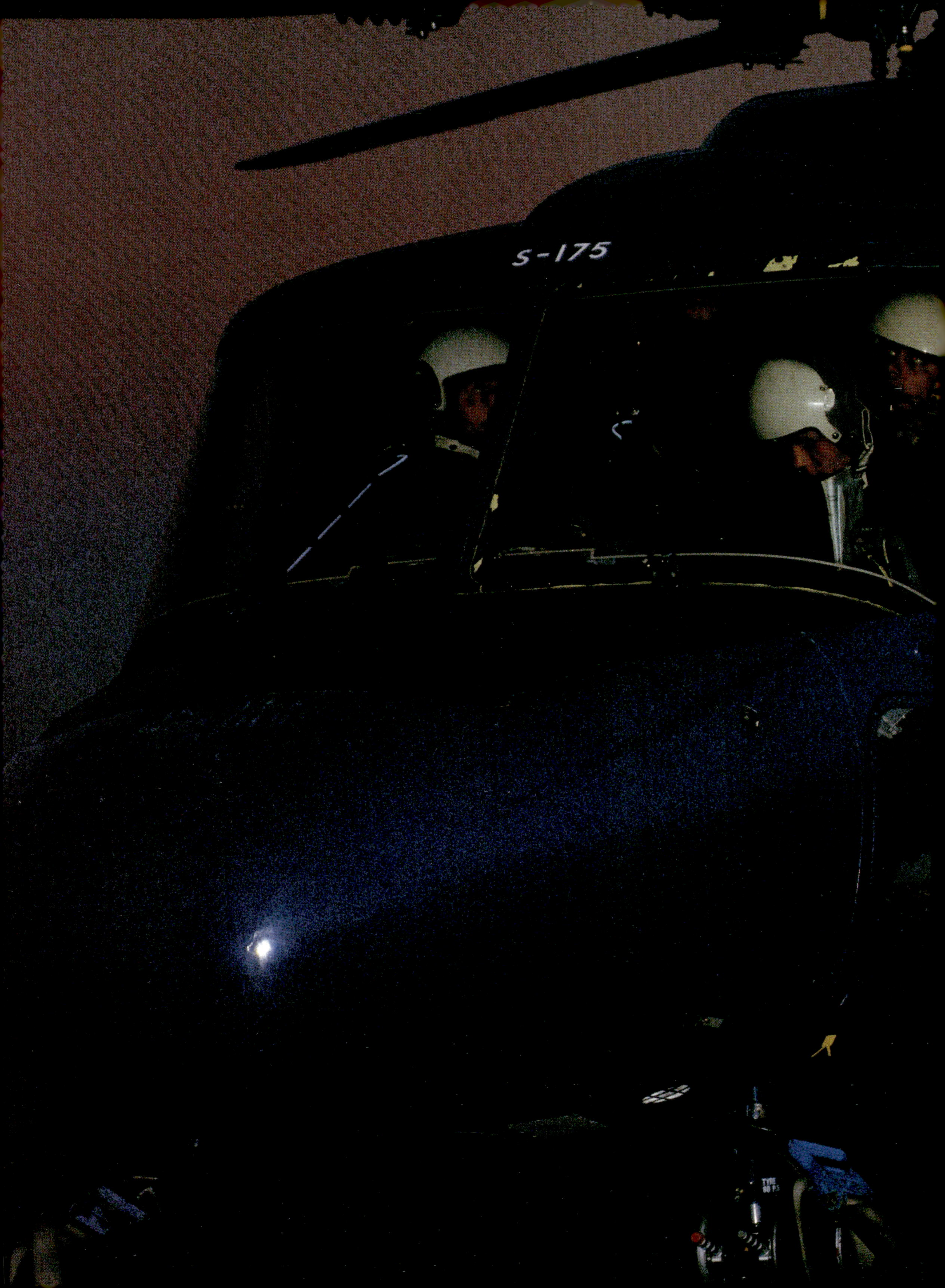
S-175

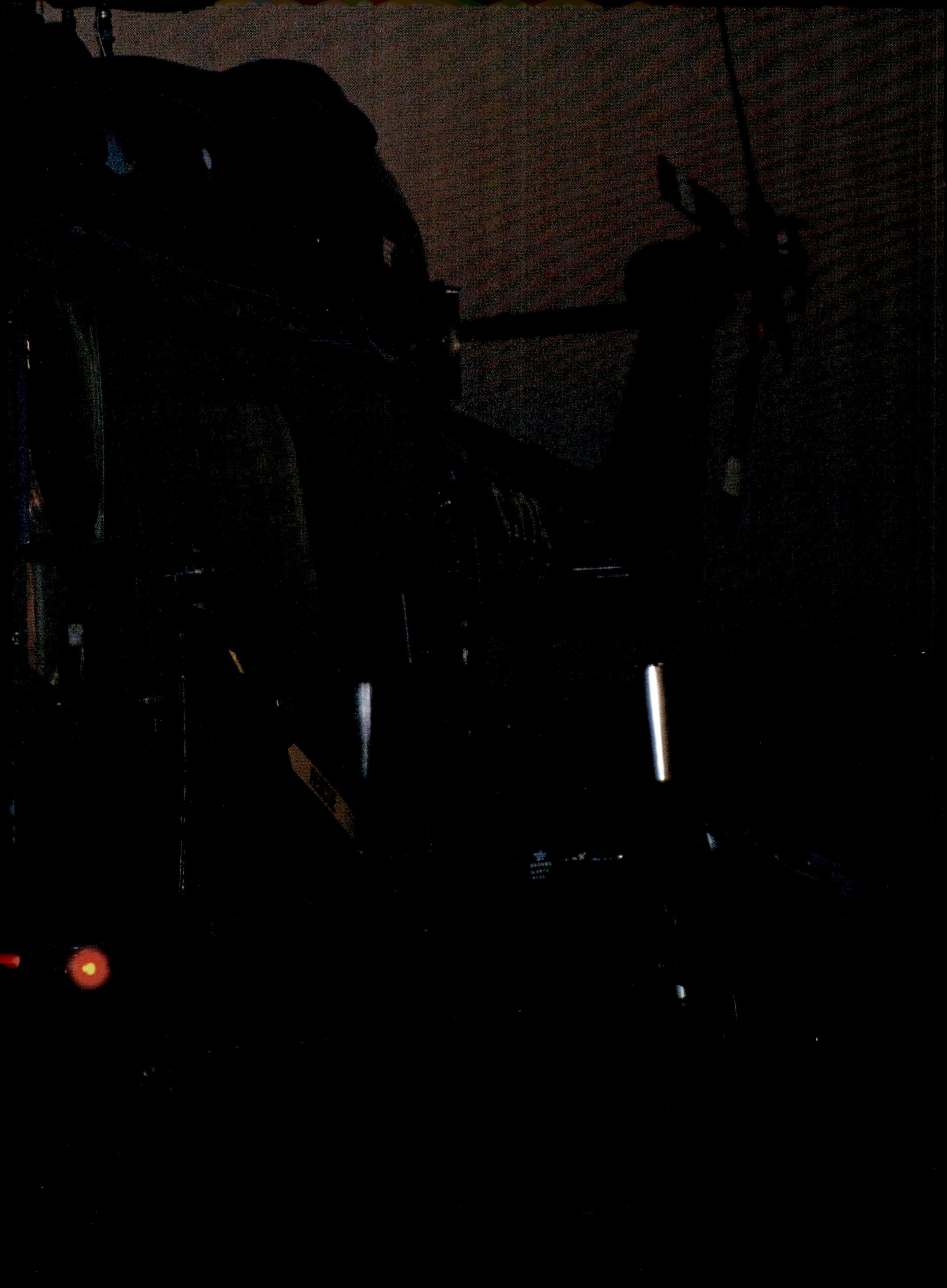

S-175

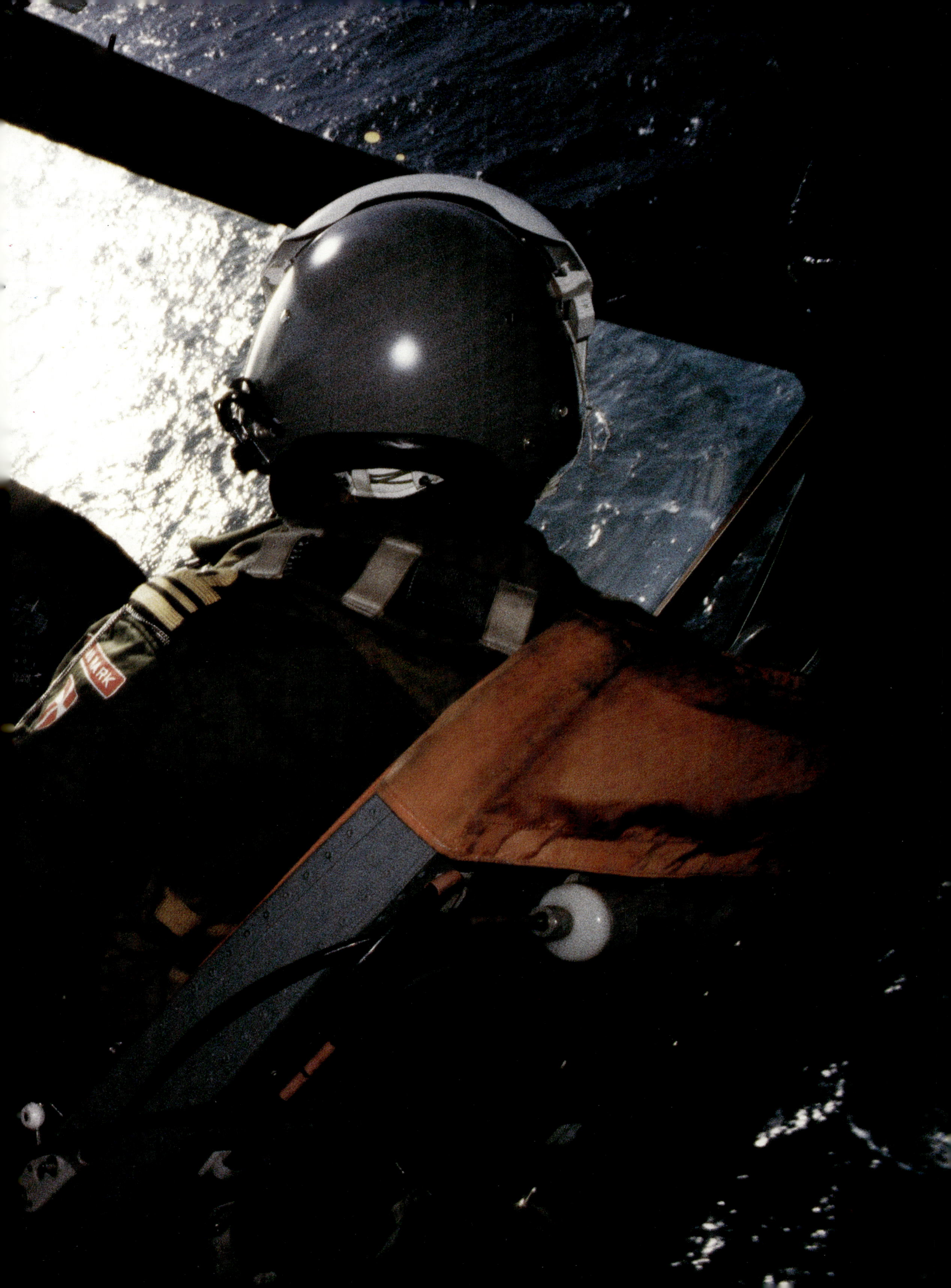

100,000 DIFFERENT PIECES FLYING IN FORMATION!

Its predecessor bombed Berlin during WWII, and its four engines come from the same factory which produced the legendary Spitfire. Since then, half a century has passed; a considerable amount of time considering that the history of military aviation spans just 80 years.

To today's youth, it is a large, unwieldy bomber with an antiquated tail wheel know only from war films and tv movies. "A memory from a distant war, of faceless British bombing crews that risked their lives against the superior Luftwaffe."

Today, the seemingly outdated bomber is still flying. Its reservations at the country's aviation museums have been cancelled. In this world of microchips, radar missiles, and color tv's there is still a place for this old boy.

It is called the Shackleton, son of the legendary Lancaster bomber. It was born during WWII, in the haste demanded by war, and outfitted with a radar system the Americans developed to combat the Japanese in a war which ended nearly 50 years ago.

At the end of WWII it was decided to let the Shackletons remain in service until the end of the 1960s. Slow and clumsy in comparison to today's modern jet aircraft, the Shackleton continues to plod through the skies over the North Atlantic where its ancient radar scanned for Russian fighters. Such was to be the fate of the Shackleton until the modern jets took over in the 70s.

The modern jets never arrived!

The ambitions were too high, the technical difficulties too great, and the budget was too tight. As a result, eight Shackletons were diverted on their way to the museums. With them, the RAF formed No. 8 Squadron at RAF Lossiemouth, Scotland, and asked a handful of their pilots to return to the days of the propeller.

The Shackleton is NATO's oldest watchdog, reporting back to NATO nations about the daily activity in Russian airspace. They also participate in numerous NATO exercises alongside some of the world's most modern fighters. A member of the same family of planes which bombed Berlin in an effort to stop Hitler, the Shackleton now works together with today's Luftwaffe.

"We fly lower than modern airplanes and often spend hours in clouds and turbulence. We're used to getting tossed around. To use the Shackleton effectively requires the expertise born only of experience. Our radar is antique and without the enhancements of a modern system. It takes experience to extract the most from the equipment we have. As a pilot you spend hour after hour manhandling the control yoke without the benefit an autopilot. You wouldn't ask that of a modern jet jockey."

■ The Shackleton's nose gunner's seat was uncomfortably exposed in the days the old giant was made to fly in. Today, however, there aren't any Messerschmitts taking a head on the big bomber with their savage 50 caliber machine guns. In fact, today's Royal Air Force Shackletons often fly training missions with the Luftwaffe. Now the nose gunner's seat is most often used as a resting place for a tired second pilot on his way home to Lossiemouth after 14 hours over the North Atlantic.

■ The Shackleton's radar operator fights with his old, yet effective, instruments while the four-engine prop carves circles in the skies where they often operate for hours on end.

■ The noise is deafening in the old bomber, and there are often six or seven frequencies chattering at the same time in the speakers. The only communication possible onboard is by intercom.

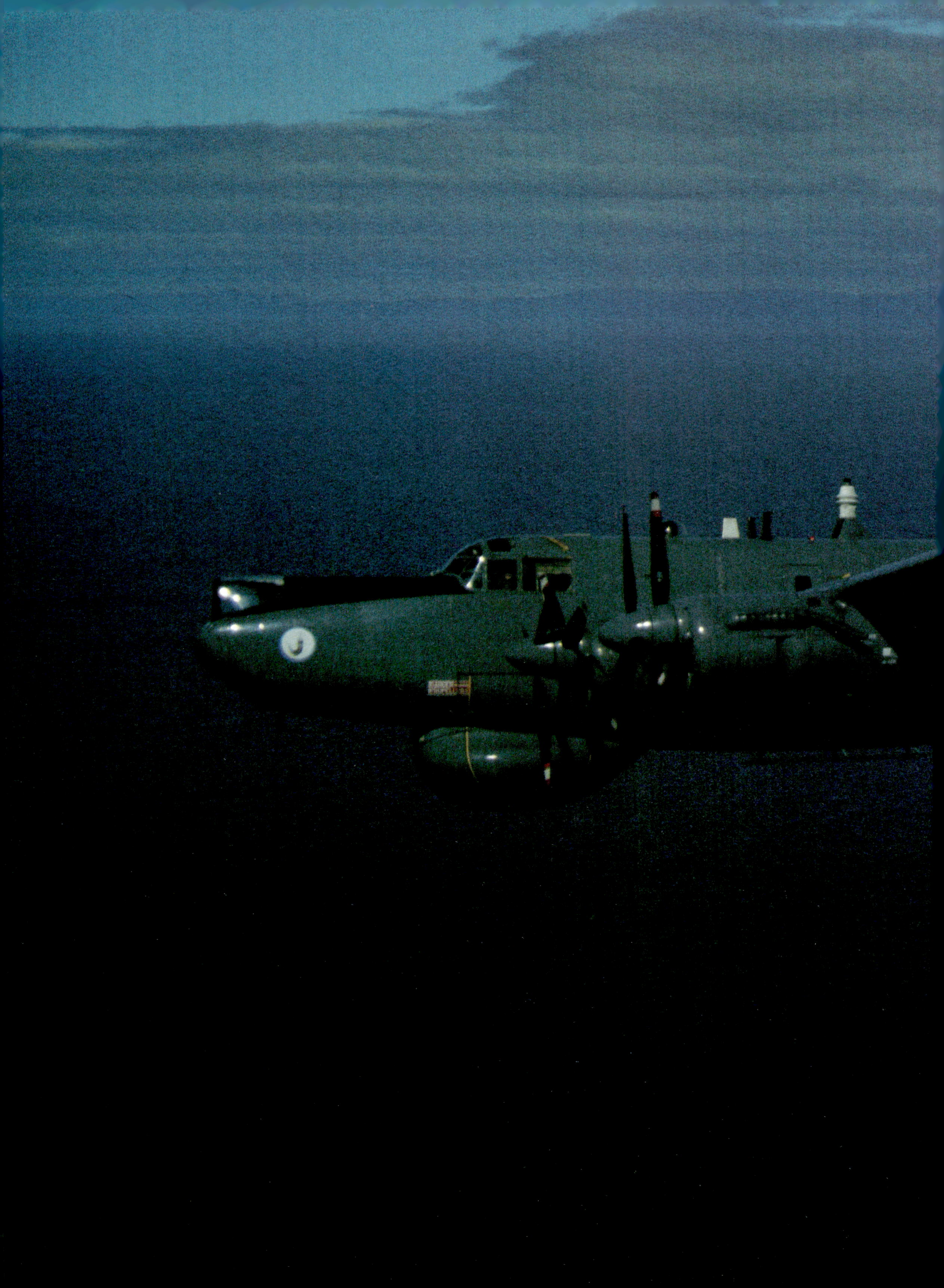

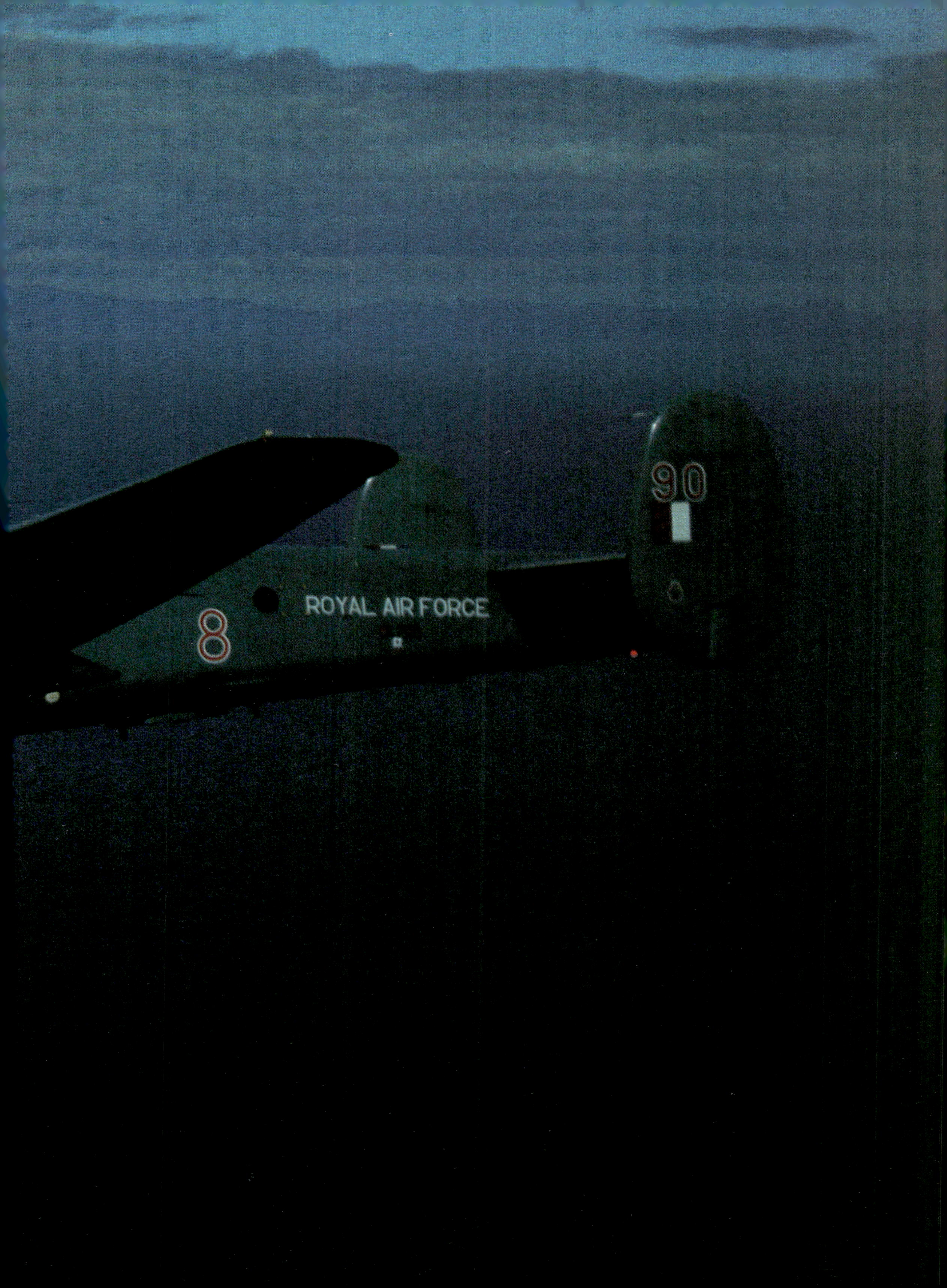
ROYAL AIR FORCE
8
90

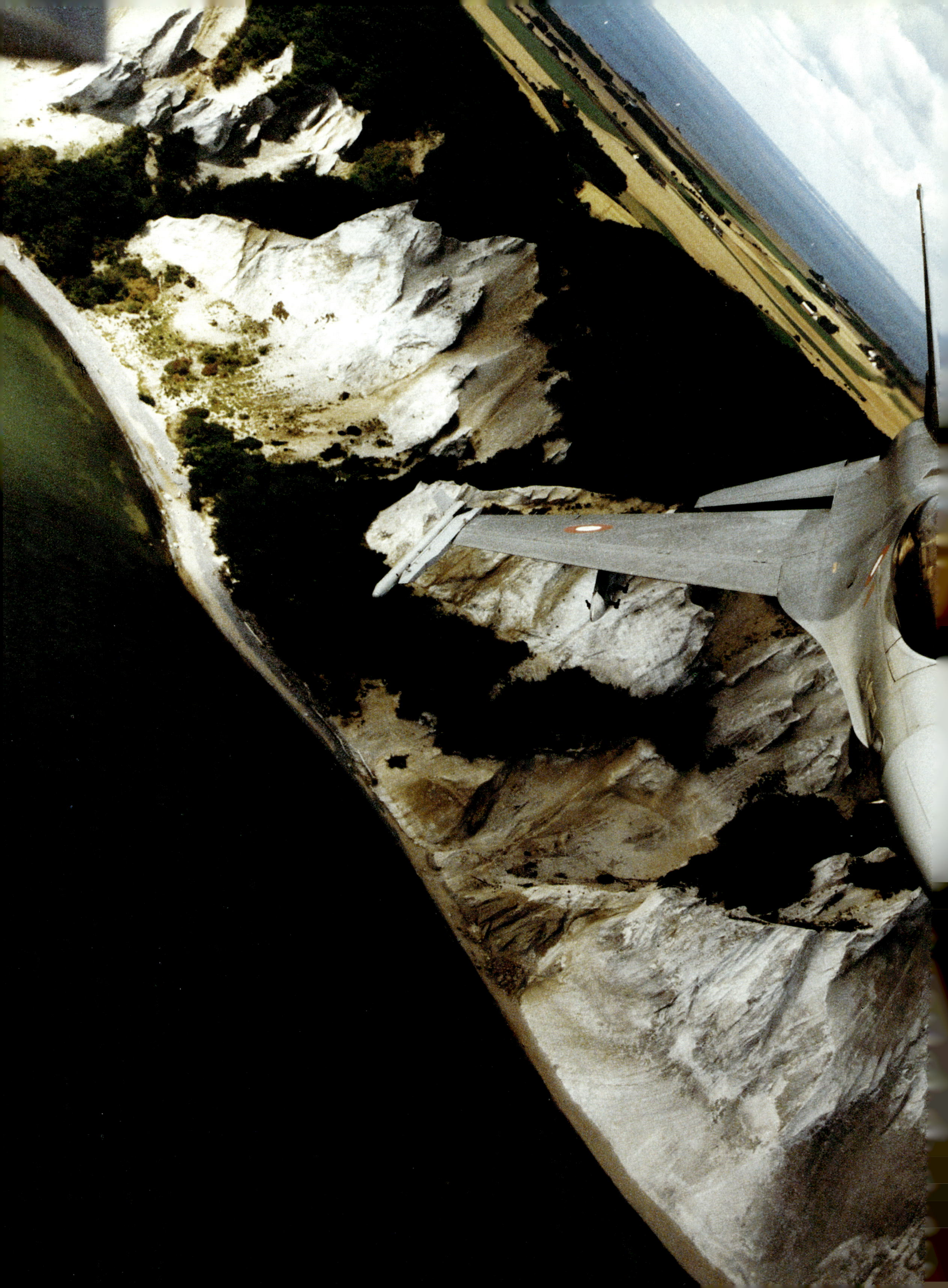

DENMARK

" *In full afterburner, I can fly from one end of Denmark to the other in 12 minutes and I mean from gear in the well at one of our western-most bases in Jutland till overhead Bornholm. At 50,000 feet and Mach 2 I can reach the island of Bornholm, Denmark's easternmost point, in 8 minutes – 1 minute more and I would be in Polish airspace so we turn over Bornholm and race westward again. A whole 15 minutes after takeoff I am back where I started from – so small is the land we guard. But for the same reasons, we are also first to the threat.*"

And a potential enemy is close to the small country made famous by H.C. Andersen. Denmark shares the Baltic Sea with Poland, East Germany, and the Soviet Union: three of the most aggressive Warsaw Pact nations. Now, if a Danish F-16 can the reach the country's most important area in 12 minutes, so can her eastern neighbors. Because of this, radar stations in Denmark get uncomfortably busy when an unknown radar return appears from the east, and that happens often.

The unknown radar return might well be one of the world's fastest bombers, the Soviet Backfire, which can approach Denmark and NATO airspace at close to three times the speed of sound. As it nears Danish airspace, the radar controller can do little more than follow it with nervous apprehension. Is it going to turn back or isn't it? The bombers can be dispersed from bases in Poland or East Germany's Baltic coast – both just minutes away. They will easily have enough fuel at takeoff to overfly Denmark and then England.

As a member of NATO, Denmark is not alone. Although the Royal Danish Air Force contributes just 60 F-16s and 30 F-35 Drakens, these will fight shoulder to shoulder with the world's best fighters on the border between East and West. The Danish Air Force has tried to maintain a low profile for many years, feeling it best not to arouse any unnecessary attention from the East. Denmark feels strongly about its participation in NATO. In keeping with that, it allows only the very best to fly its fighters. The Danish Air Force selects just 40 individuals each year from a field of 2,000 applicants to attend pilot training. Of those 40, 20 will do well enough to be sent abroad and continue with jet training which takes place at NATO's joint jet pilot training center at Sheppard Air Force Base in Wichita Falls, Texas, USA.

The Danish pilots start with the Cessna T-37 and progress to the Northrop T-38, which is very similar to the F-5 Freedom Fighter many of the neighboring Norwegian pilots will fly when they return to Norway. After one year of training in the USA, they receive their pilots wings and return home – to a new type of schooling.

(Continued on page 78)

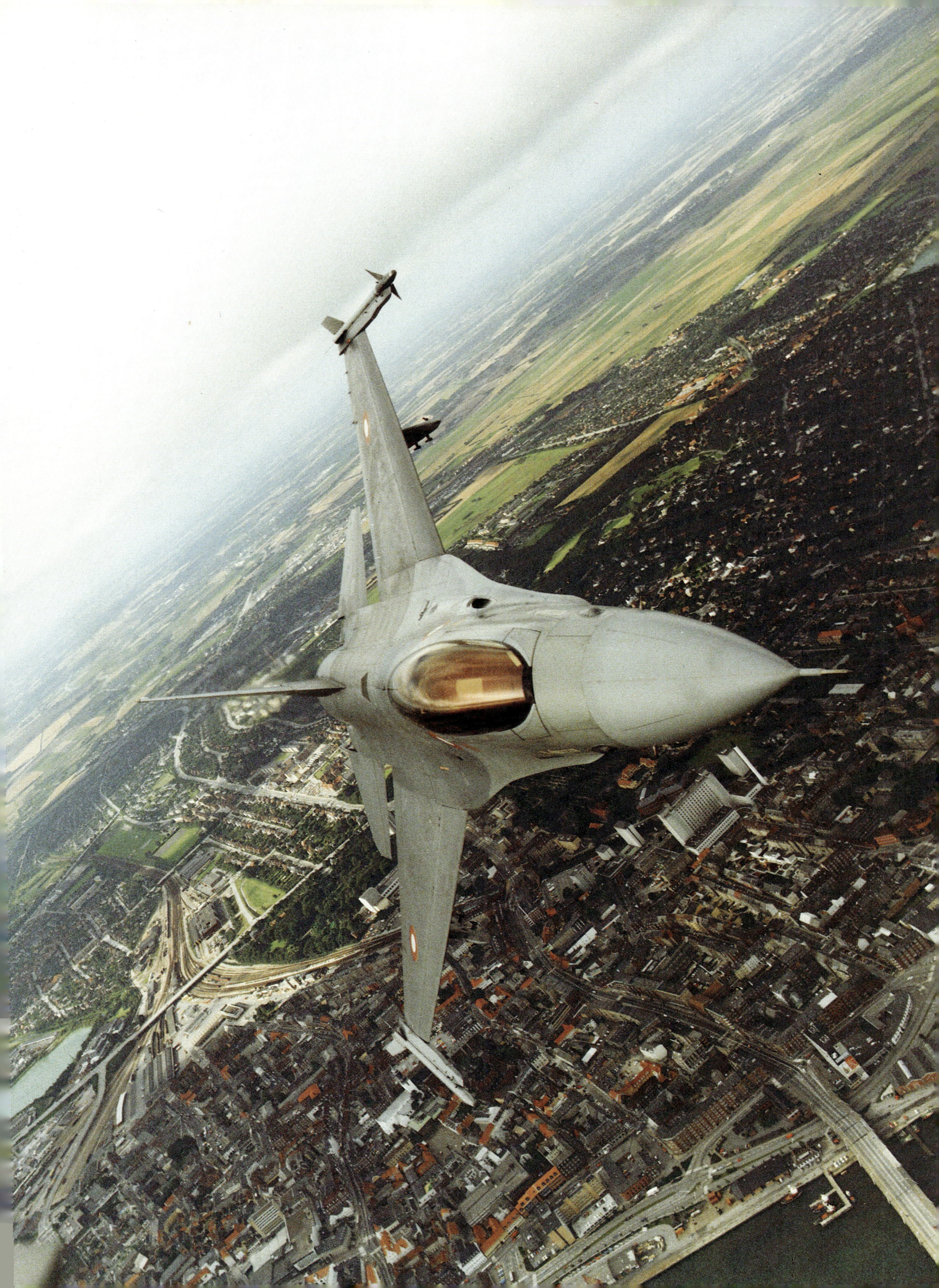

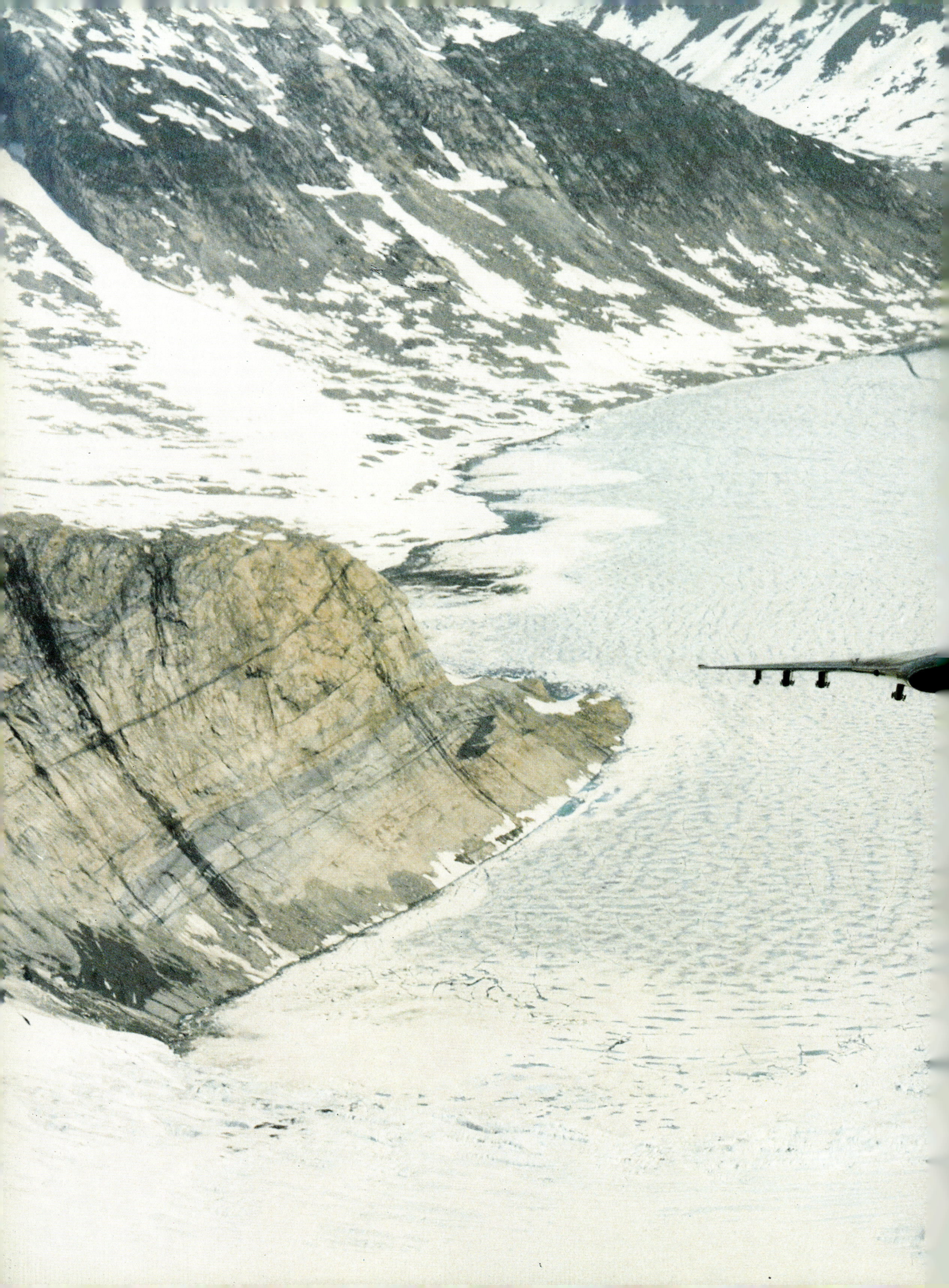

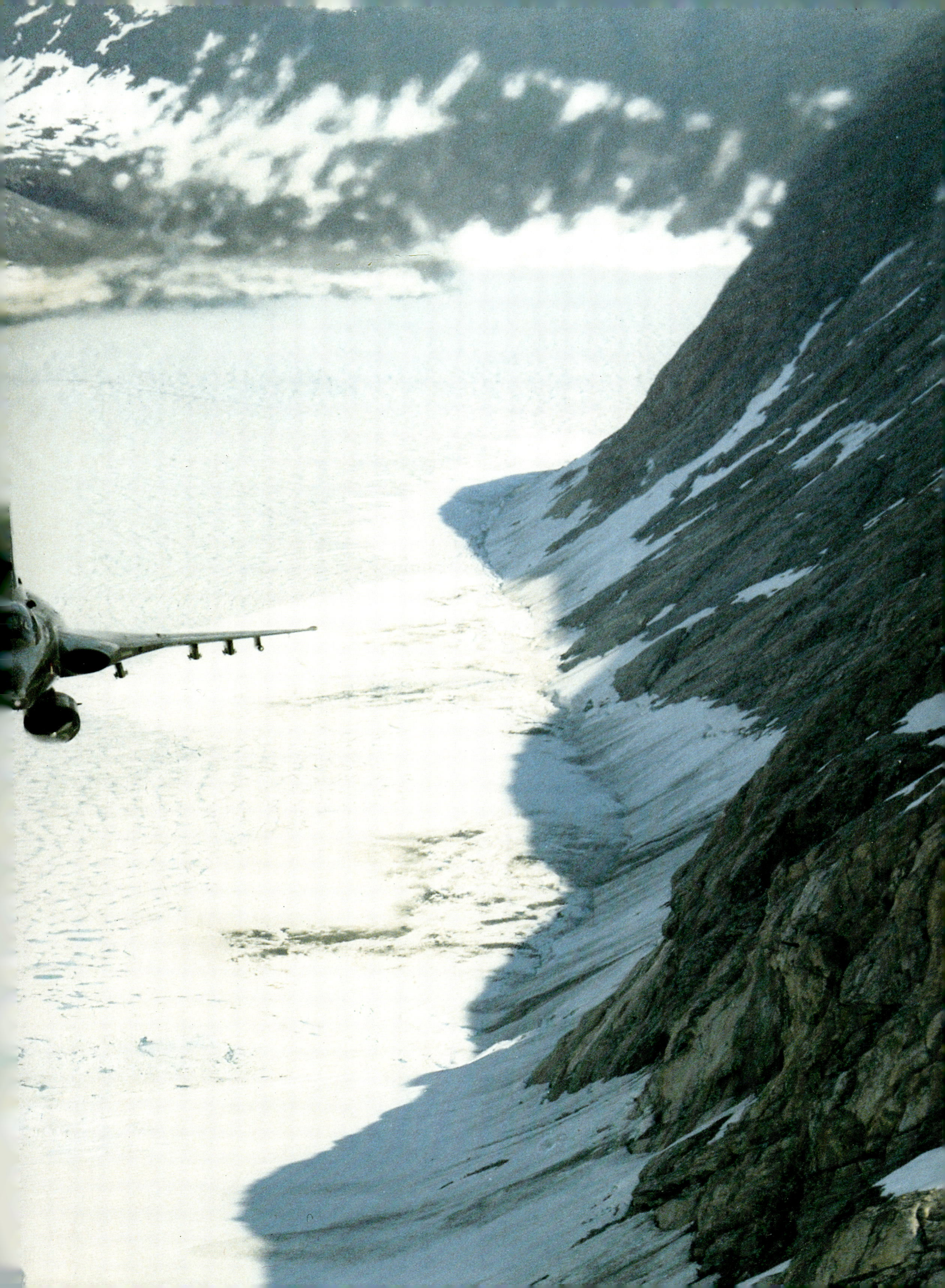

(Continued from page 74)

They will now learn to fly and fight in the F-16 or the Draken. It is here they will begin to develop the skills which set them apart from other pilots. Even at this late stage, more will be weeded out before their four year journey is over. It is only after this demanding process has been successfully completed that he is ready to fly operationally as a fully qualified fighter pilot.

If one day all Hell breaks loose it will be these few young men in their jets, the same jets which give rise to almost daily noise complaints, that will be first to take the battle to the enemy. An invasion from the Eastern Bloc will first pass through Denmark en route to England. When this happens the rest of NATO's countries will no doubt have their hands full with the border between East and West Germany. Nor will NATO partner Norway be able to help. They will be busy defending their airspace in the North. The Danish fighter squadrons will be on their own for quite a while before support arrives from England. Regardless of their ability, they won't be able to win over such a superior force. Their mission is to delay – and they will pay for that with their lives.

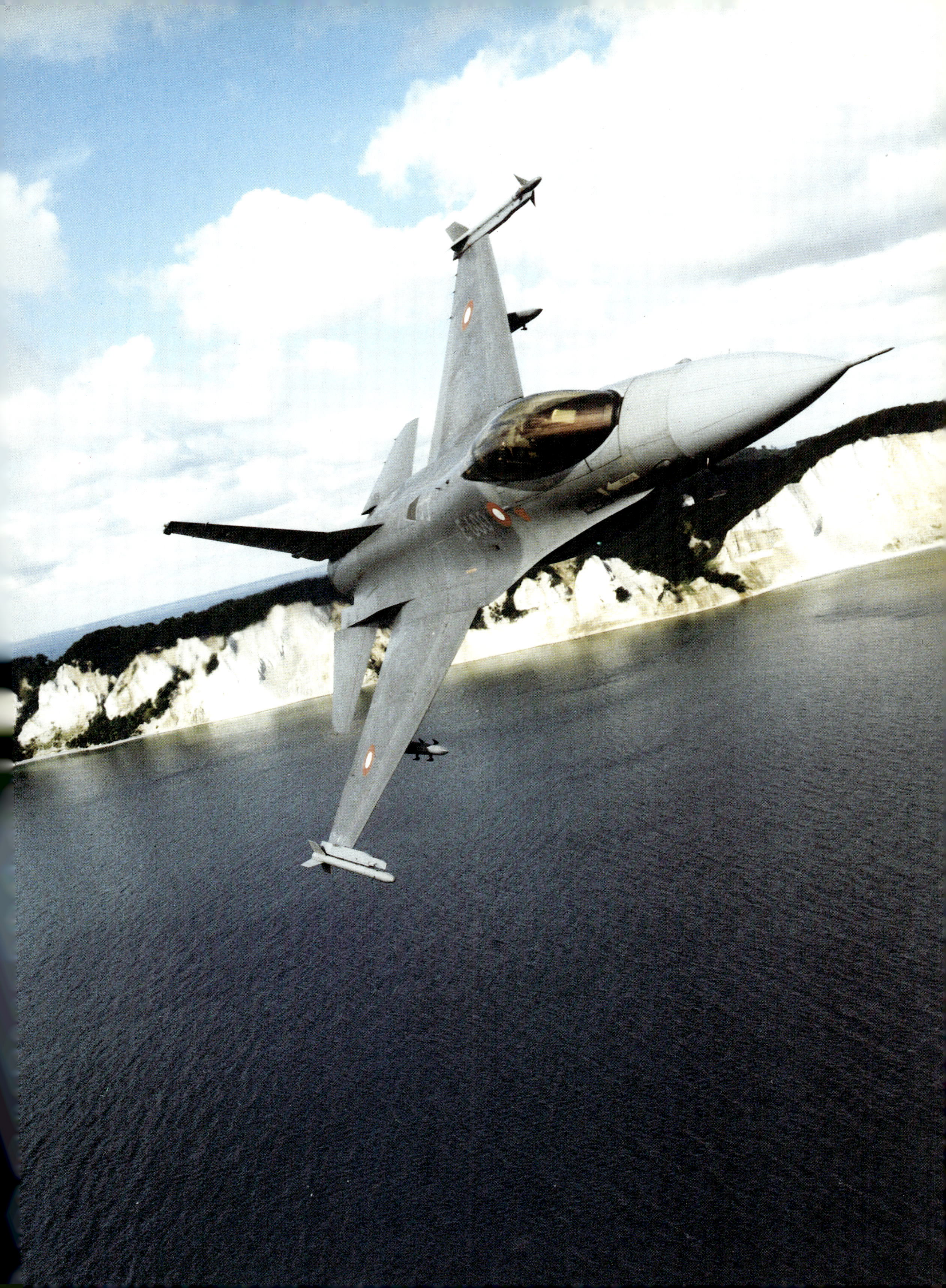

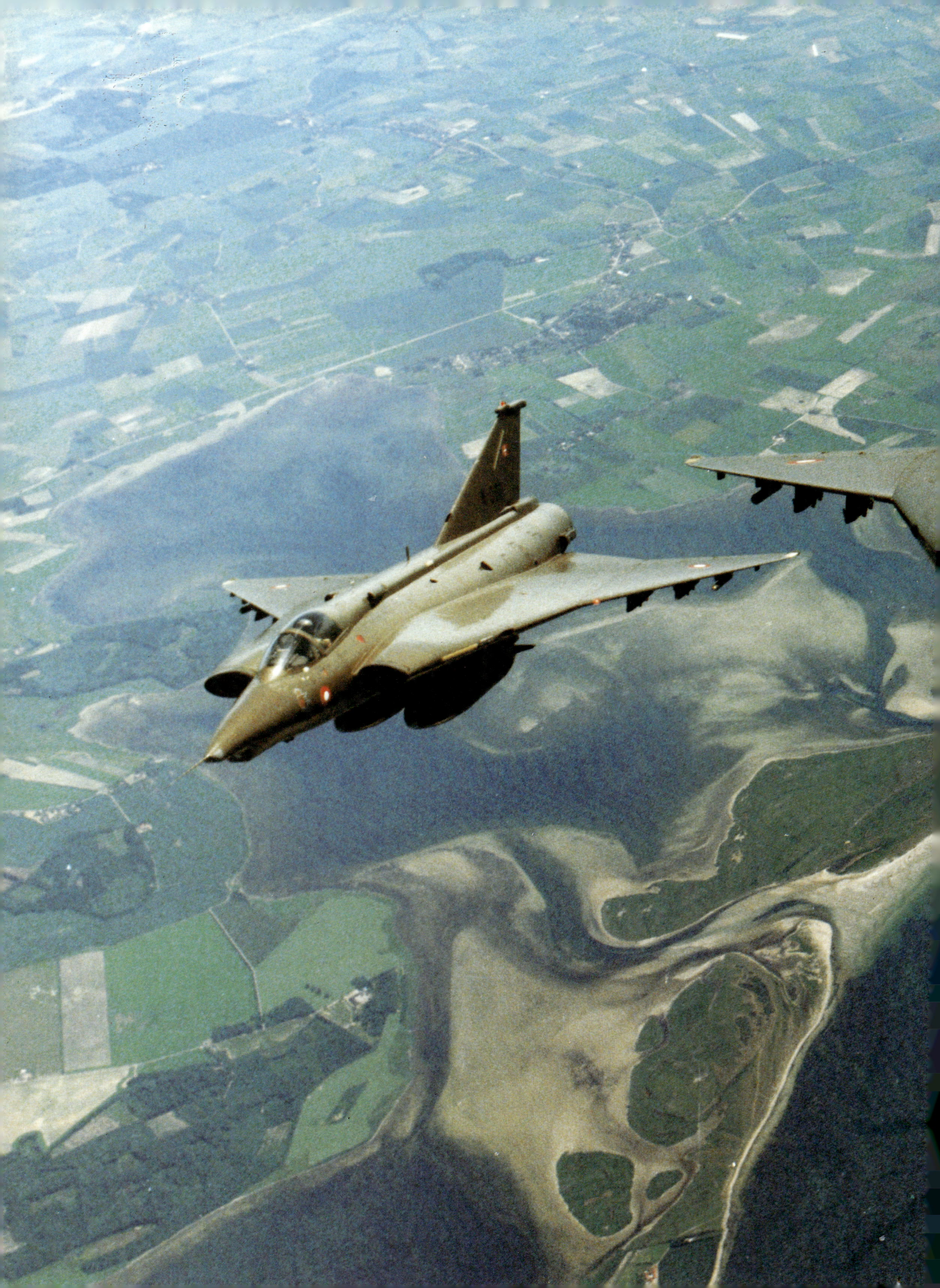

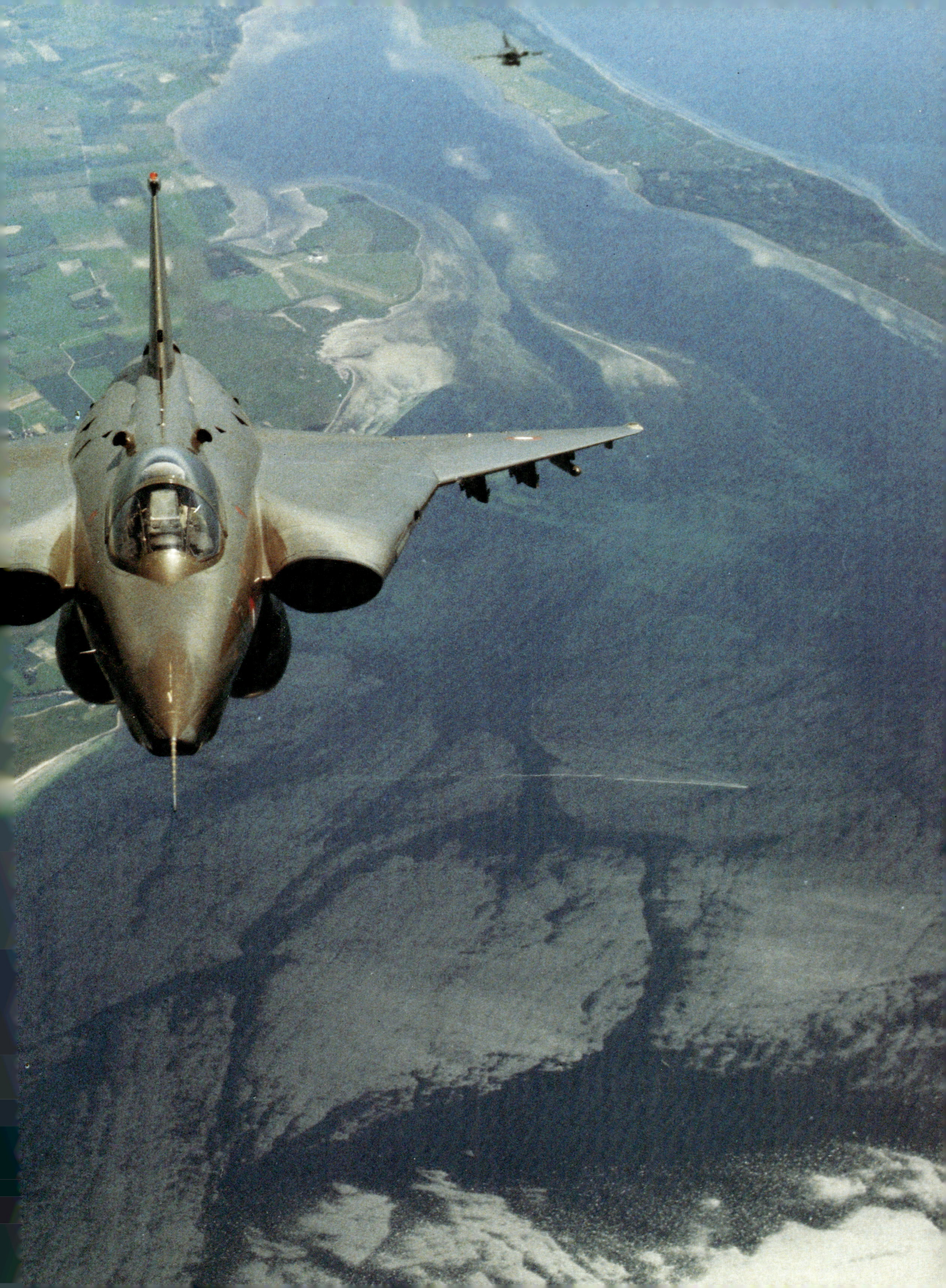

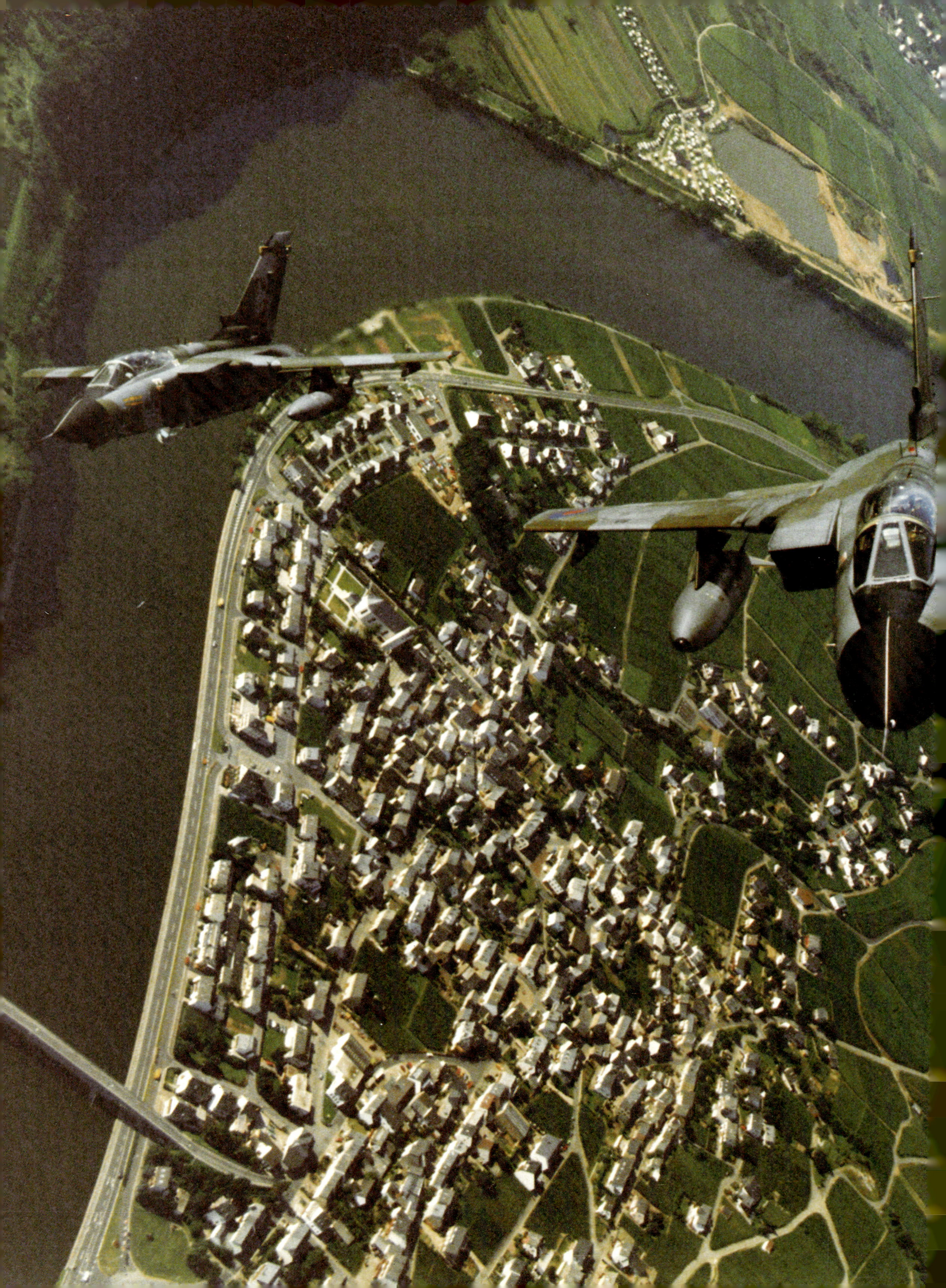

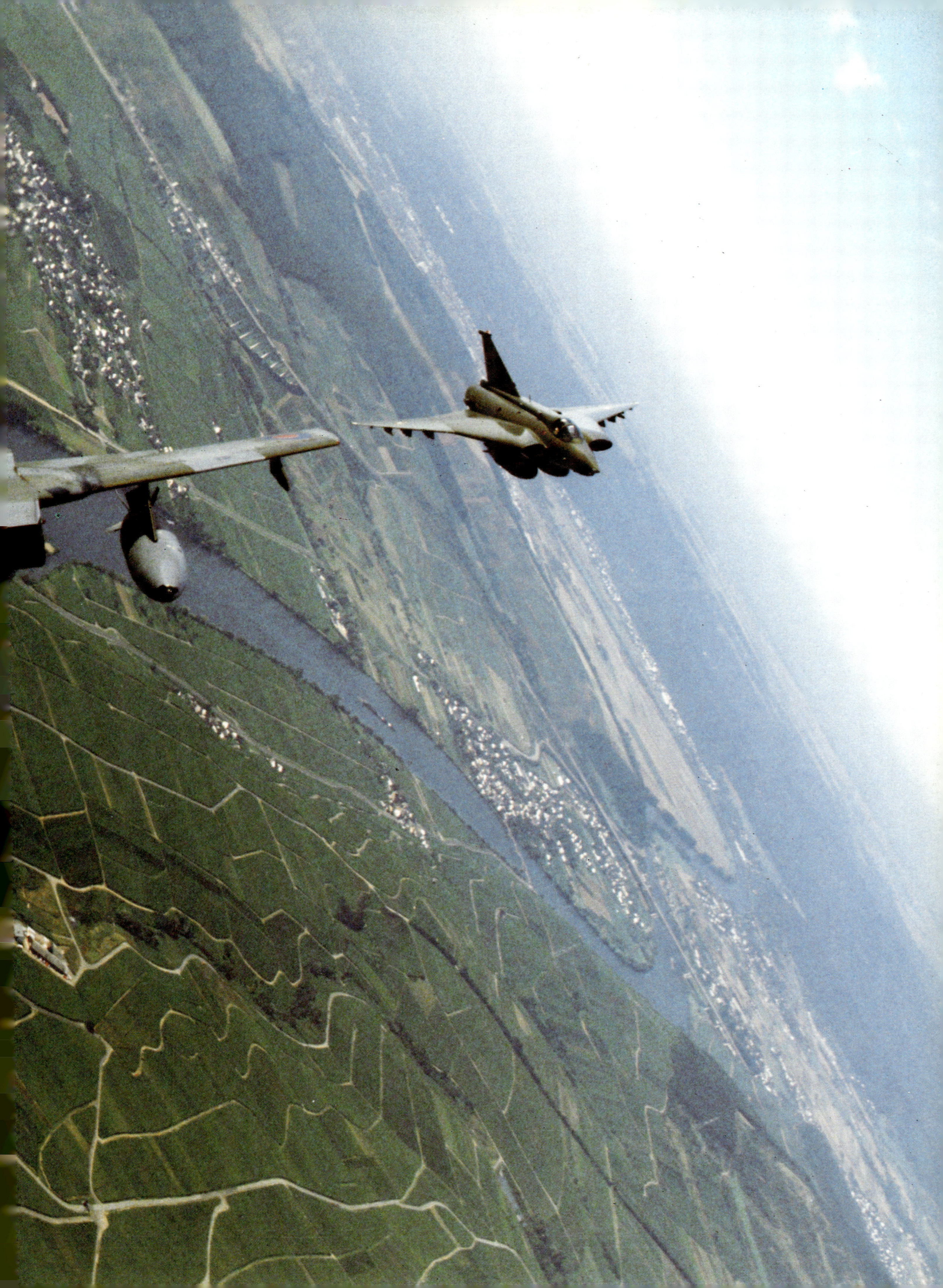

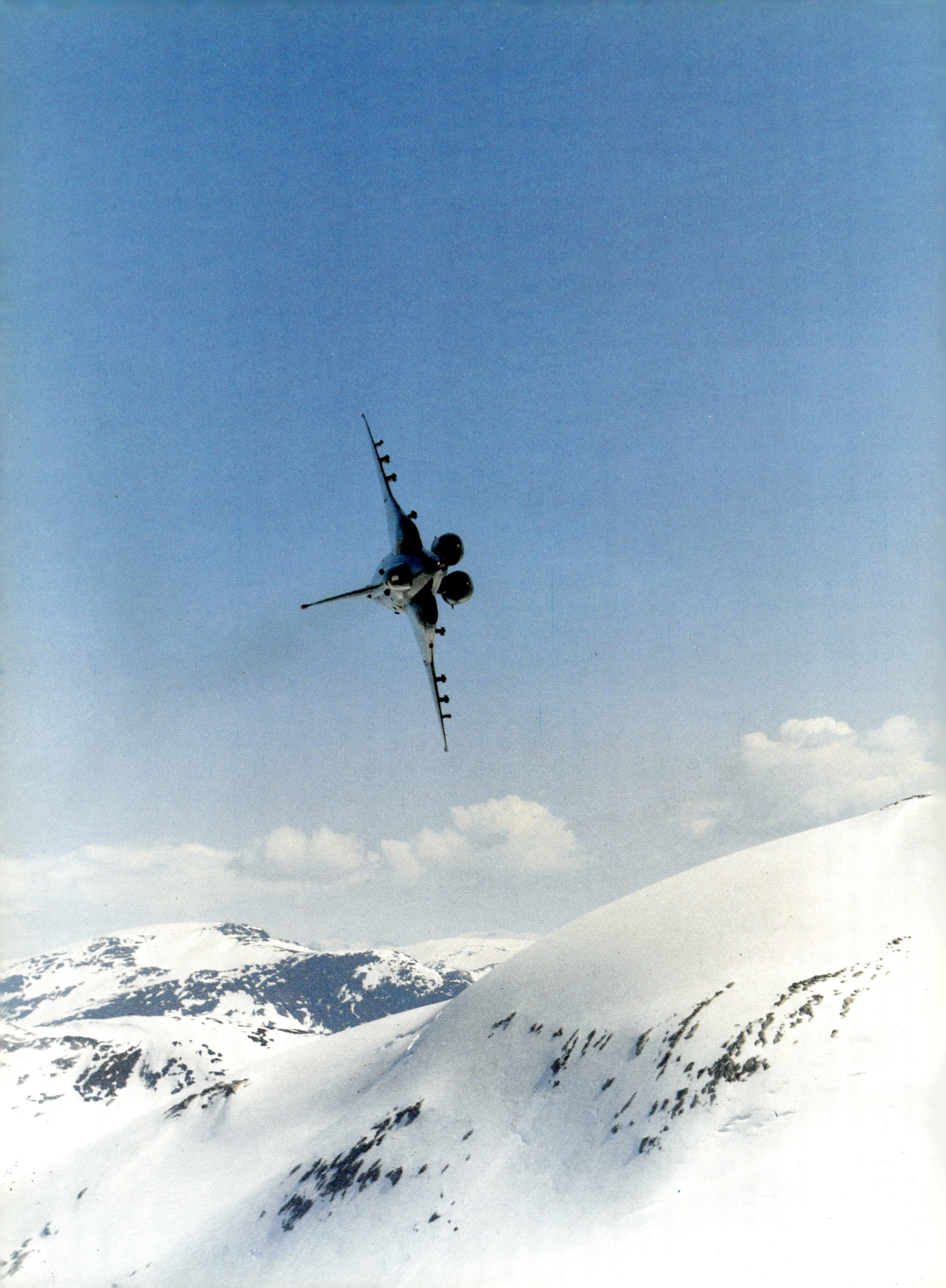

Although Denmark is a small country, its membership in NATO makes it part of a force to be reckoned with. Danish fighters frequently participate in international training exercises. On the previous page is a lone Danish Draken over the impressive Norwegian terrain. The picture was taken by its wingman with a special camera mounted under the airplane. The same camera was used to photograph dogfights over West Germany, where a Tornado attempted to get away from a Danish Draken. With the Danish Draken firmly "trapped" at 6 o'clock the West Germans should be glad that this is just training.

- Two million hours!
- 120,000,000 minutes…
- At speeds near 650 mph, that equates to an unbelievable 1.4 billion miles – to the sun and back seven times.

That is the distance which General Dynamics F-16 Fighting Falcons have logged in the skies of the world. It was a Danish F-16 from Skrydstrup Airbase which was chosen to accomplish this impressive milestone. To commemorate this important event "2,000,000 HOURS" was painted on the fuselage and wings of a Danish F-16 and a young Flight Lieutenant was given the honor of taking the Fighting Falcon on a celebration ride over Denmark's cities. On his return to Skrydstrup, a series of aileron rolls marked the start of the next million hours – almost ten years to the day that the F-16 first became operational in the 388th Tactical Fighter Wing at Hill Air Force Base, Utah, USA. Today, the F-16 can be found in the skies over the entire western world and is NATO's first choice when it comes to short range strike missions. It is perfect for a small country like Denmark, where it is possible to inspect and protect the entire country's airspace on one single mission.

87

■ From Skrydstrup Airbase on the Jutland peninsula of Denmark, to Nellis Air Force Base in Las Vegas, Nevada, they followed the track which their Viking ancestors took a millenium ago. The trip of today's Vikings included five stops at various desolate locations along the northern rim of the Atlantic and many hours in the somewhat cramped cockpits of their F-16s. Hours of breathing through an oxygen mask, surrounded by instruments, and fighting to stay in position only a few feet from your wingman; yet, to the man, every Danish pilot would gladly do it again in an instant!

■ The "bad guys" in any Red Flag exercise at Nellis are the USAF Aggressors flying the Northrop F-5. The Aggressors are chosen from among the most experienced fighter pilots in the USAF. Painted like Russian fighters, except for the red star on their tails, the Aggressors were the model for the adversaries of the US Navy's Top Gun program in San Diego – made famous by the movie of the same title.

RETURN OF THE VIKINGS

■ The United States' Grand Canyon lies majestically beneath a formation of F-16 Fighting Falcons. But these F-16s don't have USAF markings on the fuselage. These four jets have just finished a gruelling flight over the cold waters once ruled by their forefathers, the Vikings. The Royal Danish Air Force participated in one of the world's most demanding military exercises, Red Flag, which is held over the Nevada desert north of Nellis Air Force Base. Red Flag is an attempt to create as realistic an airwar exercise as is possible. It brings fighter pilots and their machines from all over the free world together in unfamiliar surroundings; forcing everyone to overcome their cultural and linguistic barriers in order to work together towards a common objective.
The flight from Denmark to Las Vegas passed over Iceland, Greenland, and Newfoundland, actually the same course the Vikings sailed over 1000 years ago.

" How does a man who starts a world war feel? I was close to knowing once. The actions and events which led up to the whole thing were pure routine; I just carried out my job. The world was scarcely closer to war without actual fighting than after my mission that day.

I was a fighter pilot in the Danish Air Force and flew the RF-84F, a magnificent fighter, the F-16 of its day. I was flying a routine photo reconnaissance mission over the North Sea, cruising along at 30,000 feet when the radar controller called me. I remember the words distinctly: my callsign and then 'We have a Russian freighter just north of Skagen'. Nothing out of the ordinary there, we have many sailing by Skagen every day as the Russians use Danish waters to sail out from the Baltic. But radar continued: 'Fly close to him, we need a picture of his deck'. Well, I followed radar's directive and shortly afterwards intercepted the freighter. I made a low pass and let the camera run. Normally, seamen on deck wave as you race by, but not here. The ship seemed deserted. I didn't see a single person. The cargo was also unusual. Everything appeared to be covered by large pieces of tarpaulin. I felt it might be important and decided to make one more pass. I then headed home to my base and let the technicians get the film from the fighter's camera.

– Enlargement and photo analysis showed the freighter had missiles on board. Their destination was Cuba, where the Russians were building a ballistic missile sight just minutes' flight from American soil. With the pictures as proof, then President Kennedy warned that he would have the ship sunk if the Russians let it continue on to Cuba. The Russian freighter continued. The US Air Force went to their highest state of readiness. A final warning was given, and on the brink of a third World War, Khrushchev decided to call the ship back. I can't help thinking the whole thing began with just a routine patrol over the North Sea "

Ex-fighter pilot, RDAF

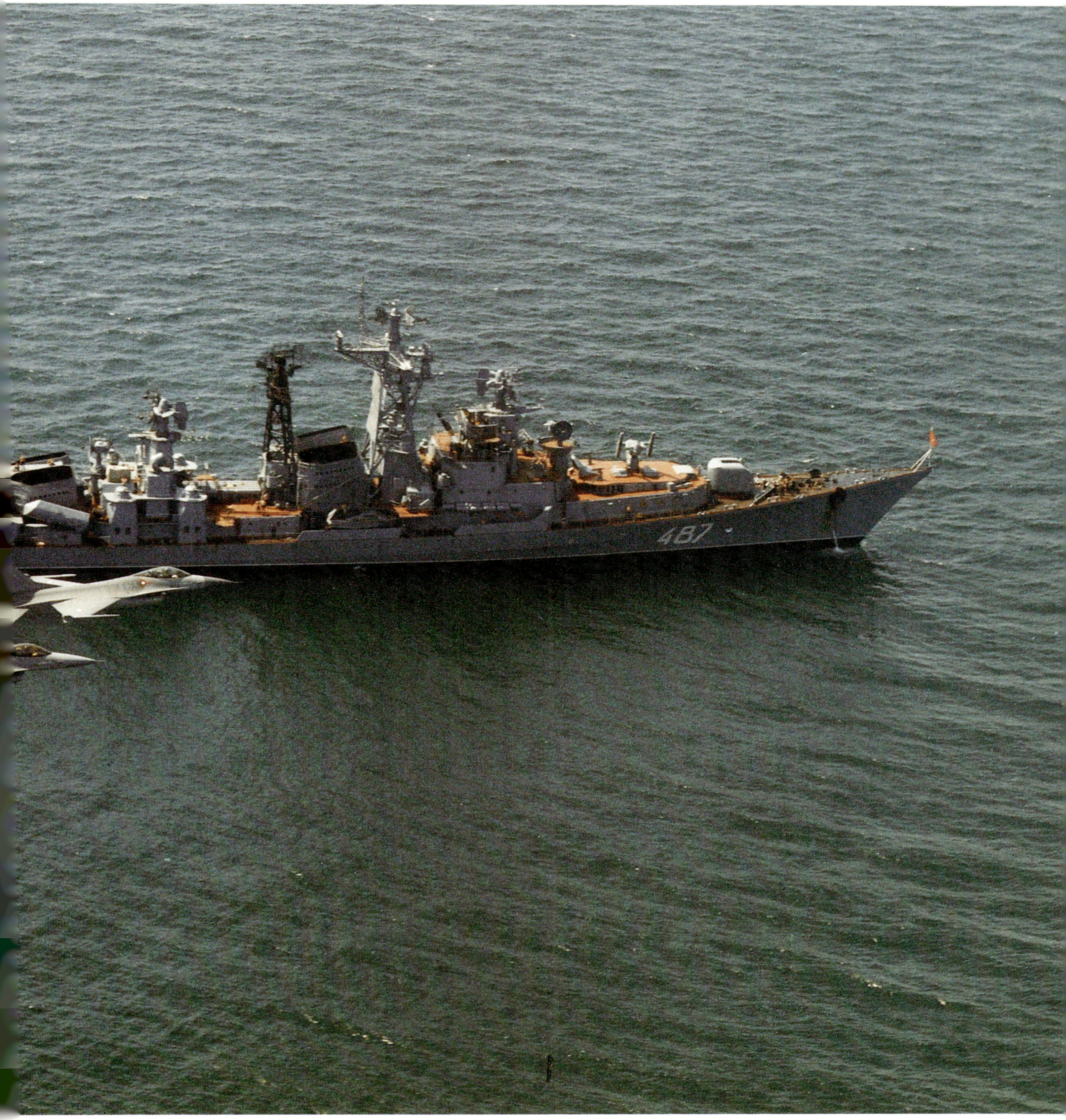
487

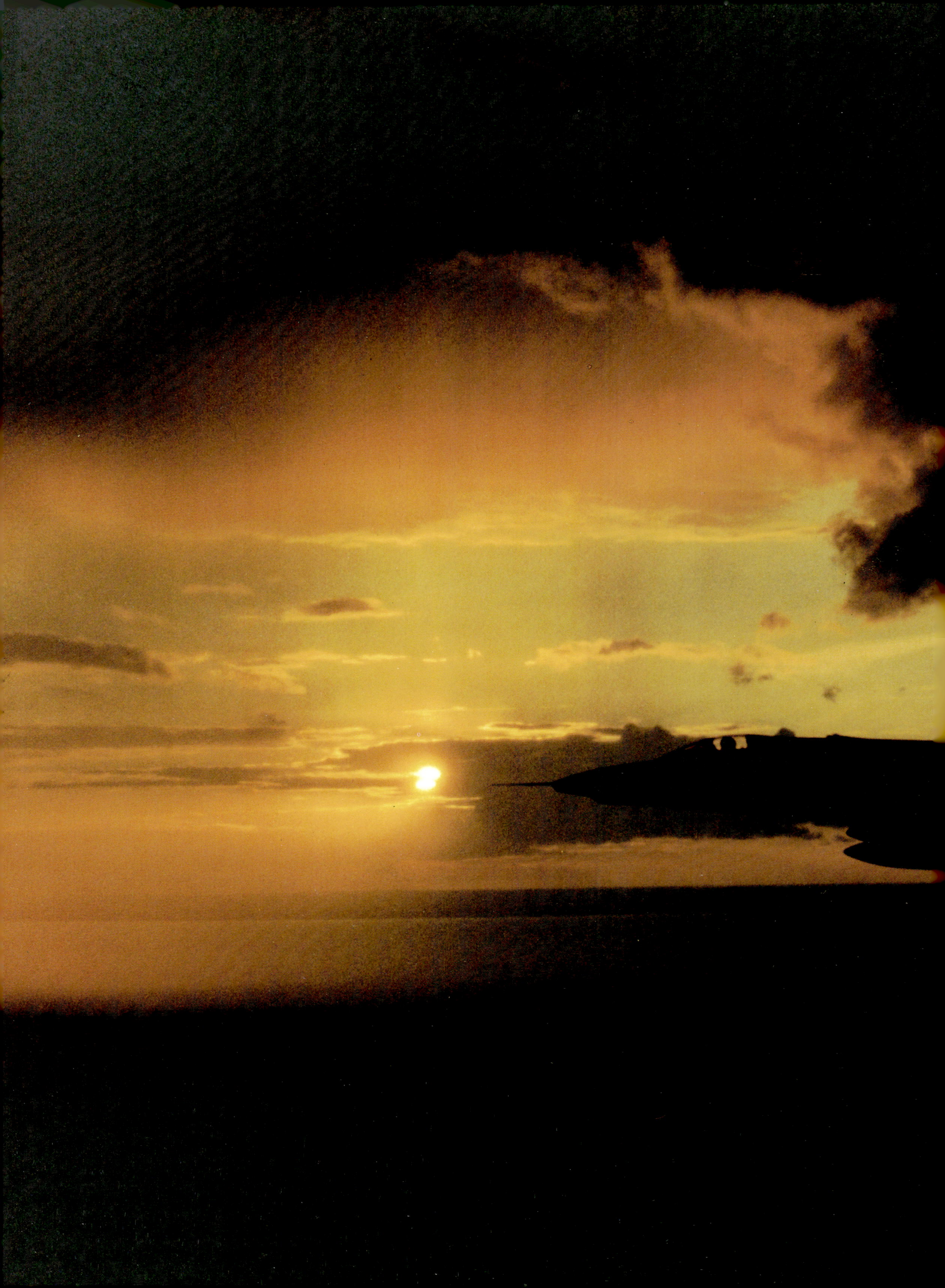

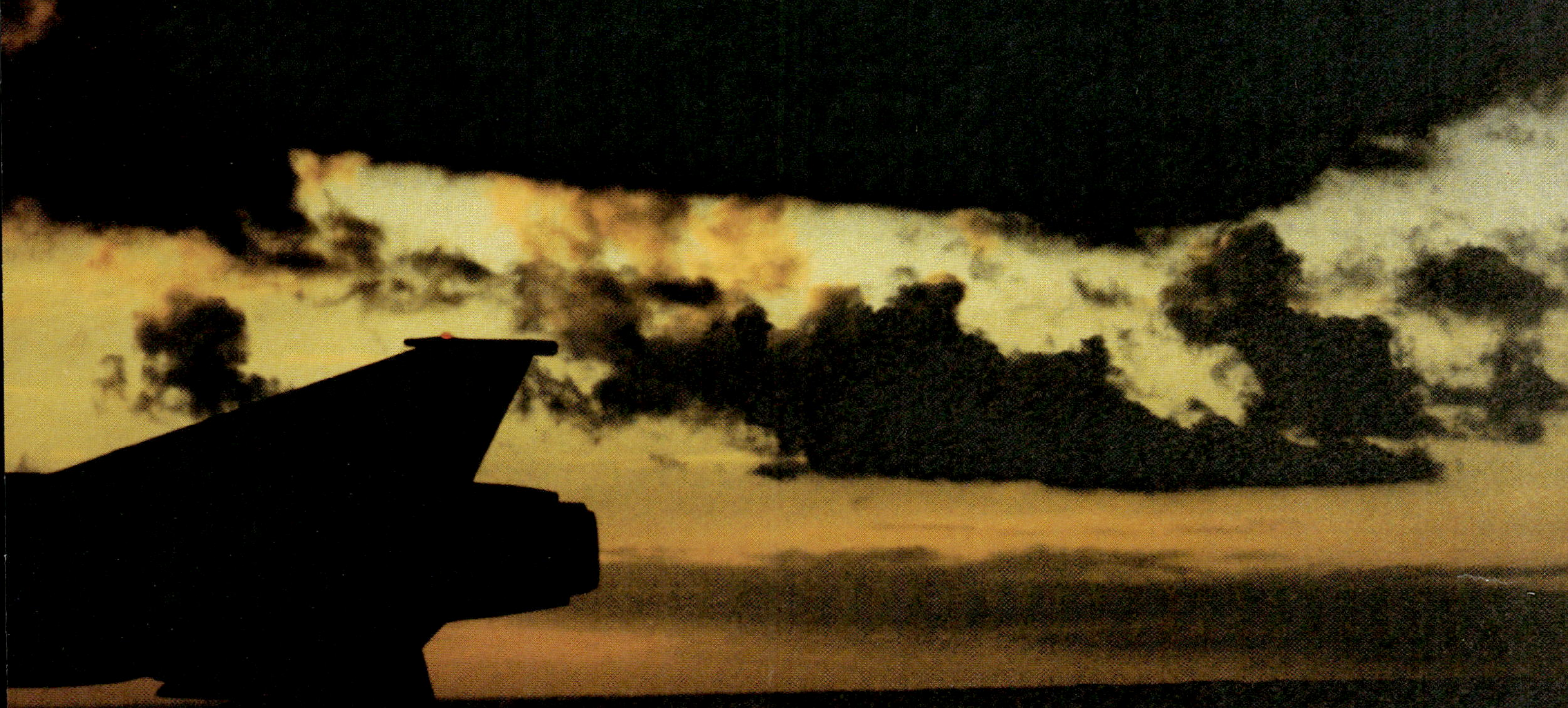

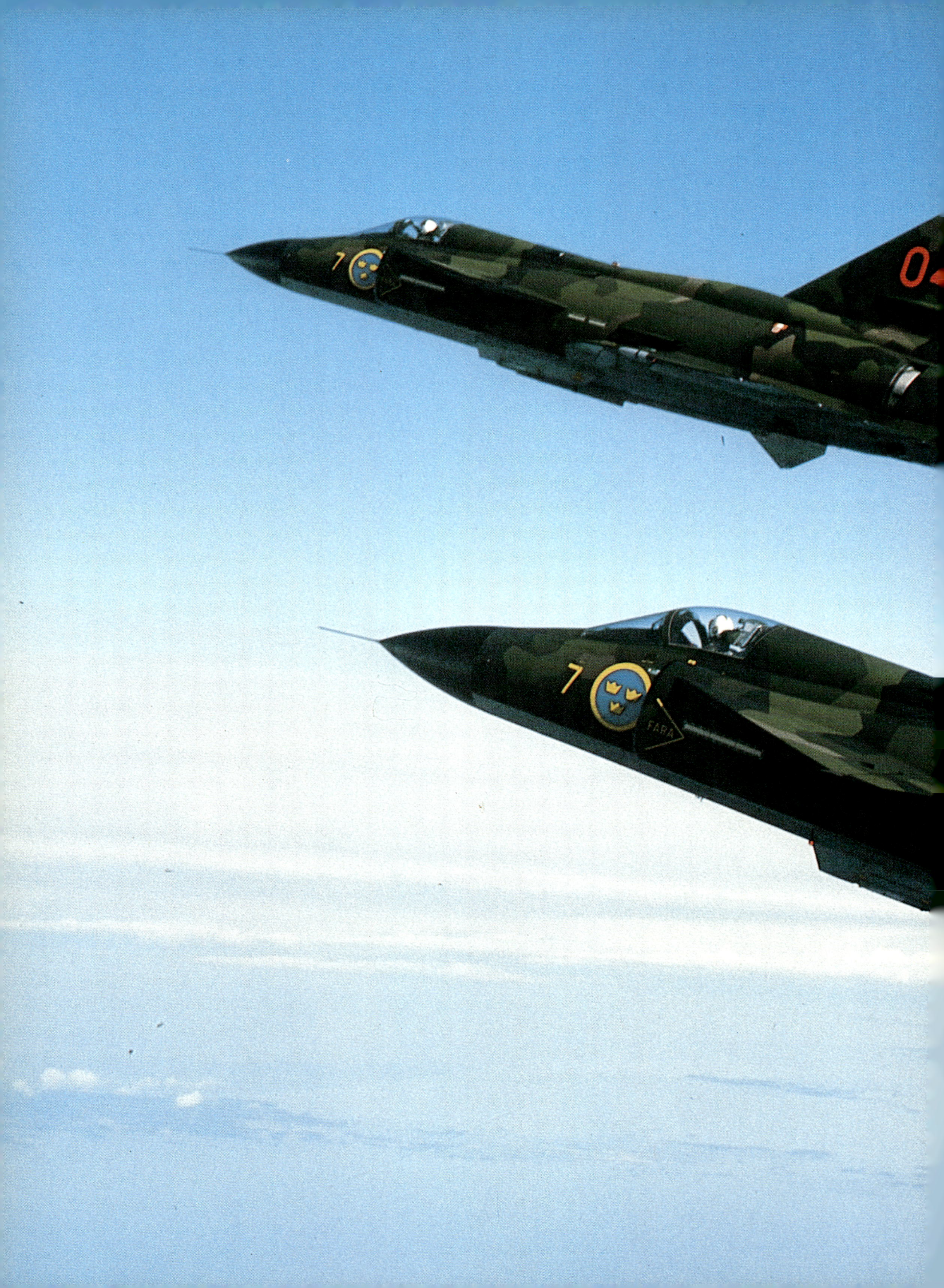
7
7
FARA

SWEDEN

There lies a country in Northern Europe which stretches 1000 miles from north to south. Its northern regions are an ice-cold wilderness, where few people have set foot. It is an unbelievably exciting and varied country – but with a smaller population than the city of London. A closely knit society, you will rarely find another which is more patriotic.

Sweden is a neutral country, having chosen not to follow its Scandinavian brothers Denmark and Norway, who joined NATO after World War II. Sweden, however, doesn't really have the same wounds to lick. They were not subject to German occupation as Norway and Denmark were, but served as a haven for refugee Jews and a large number of escaped POWs – among them many pilots from the RAF and USAF.

Neutrality notwithstanding, Sweden has known enough of war to realize how important a strong defense is. In fact, this sparsely populated country with its untamed wilderness has built up an exceptional Air Force. The Swedish Air Force doesn't operate solely from well established bases, but also from the entire Swedish highway system. All over Sweden parts of the highway system can be quickly converted into serviceable runways. There are so many possibilities in a country whose highway system covers thousands of miles that even the cleverest intelligence network would never be able to keep track of all the possible landing strips. There are just too many – and their positions can be shifted continuously.

To operate within this system requires a special fighter. A nation which builds some of the world's best cars (Saab and Volvo) and for years has ranked among the world's most highly developed societies, can naturally handle the task themselves. To satisfy the country's needs Saab's aircraft division and Volvo's engine division joined forces.

The results are called Draken, Viggen, and now Gripen.

The demands Sweden places on its fighters are extreme: they must be capable of functioning in the roles of interceptor, ground attack, fighter bomber, and reconnaissance. It is understood that they must be supersonic, beginning with the 1950's debut of the Draken on the other side of the sound barrier. This delta-winged fighter has dominated the Scandinavian skies for decades, flying in Sweden, Denmark and Finland. Today, the 30-year-old Draken operates in three countries and through continual system updates has continued to be one of the most modern fighters. During NATO exercises, Danish Drakens have often demonstrated that they can still play with the big boys, holding their own against the F-15, F-16, and F-18.

The Draken was the predecessor of the Viggen, Saab's tandem winged fighter: heavy, big, expensive, but incredibly effective. From a short highway strip surrounded by dense forests and subject to strong turbulence, its strong turbofan engine, a Volvo RM8B, literally rockets the fighter into the air. With afterburner blazing, it can climb to an altitude of 30,000 in close to 90 seconds. This formidable delta-winged fighter is built for the rugged Swedish environment and with its Mach 2 speed and formidable short takeoff and landing capability it may be among the world's most advanced fighters. Yet its only mission is to defend Sweden's skies. The Viggen was one of the favourites, before European NATO members made the arms deal of the century, buying General Dynamics F-16s instead.

Although the Viggen should continue to operate well into the next century, Sweden's future is called Gripen. The Gripen, combined attack, fighter and reconnaissance, has proved to be an extremely large project. Like the Viggen, the Gripen is a tandem winged, supersonic fighter. The development of this futuristic fighter has been hard. Its cockpit has become almost exclusively digital, divided into four large displays which provide so much information that it will take a "superpilot" to make use of it all. Nonetheless, the Gripen will be a formidable adversary for many years to come. This futuristic fighter first took to the sky in December 1988.

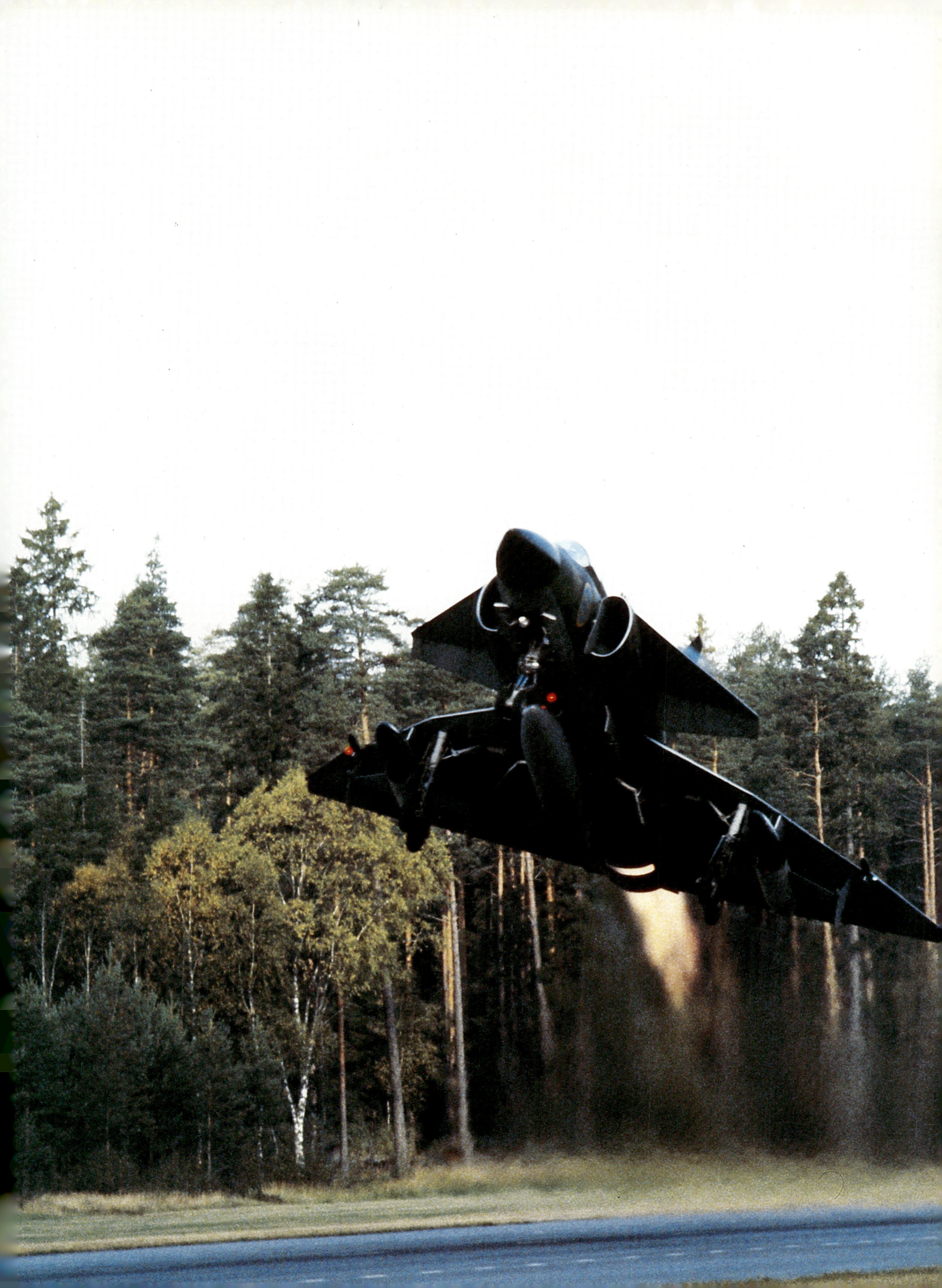

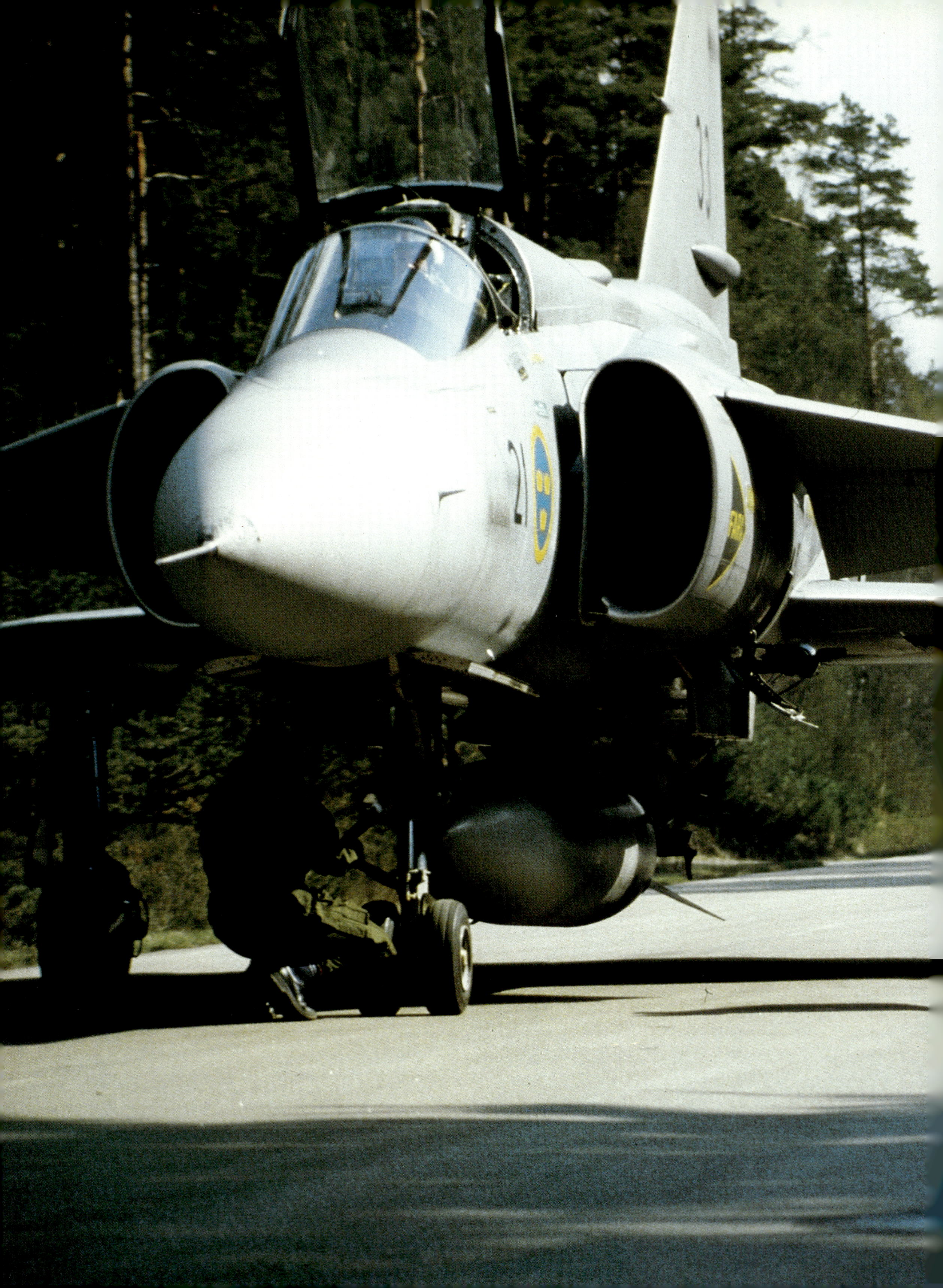
21

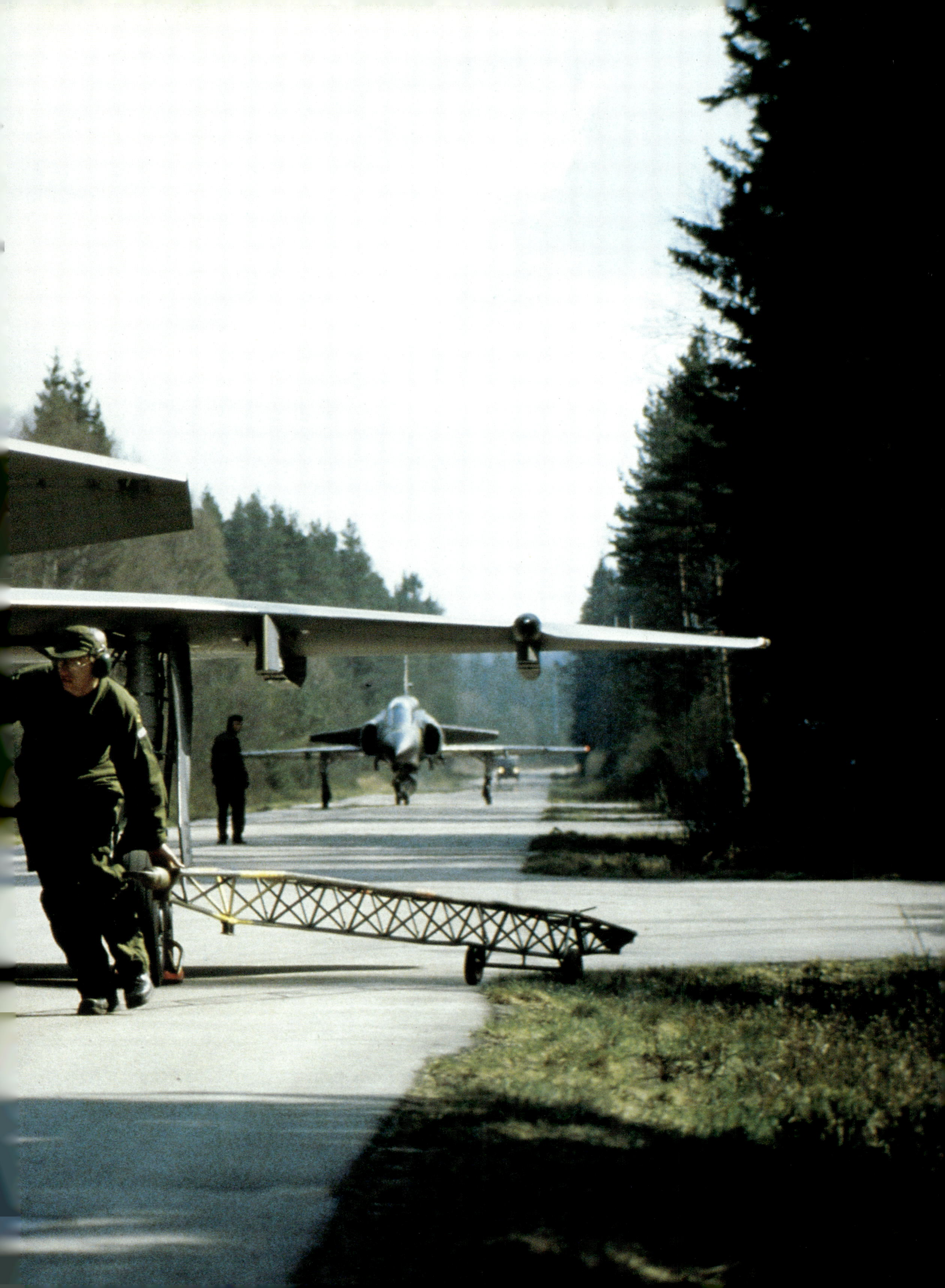

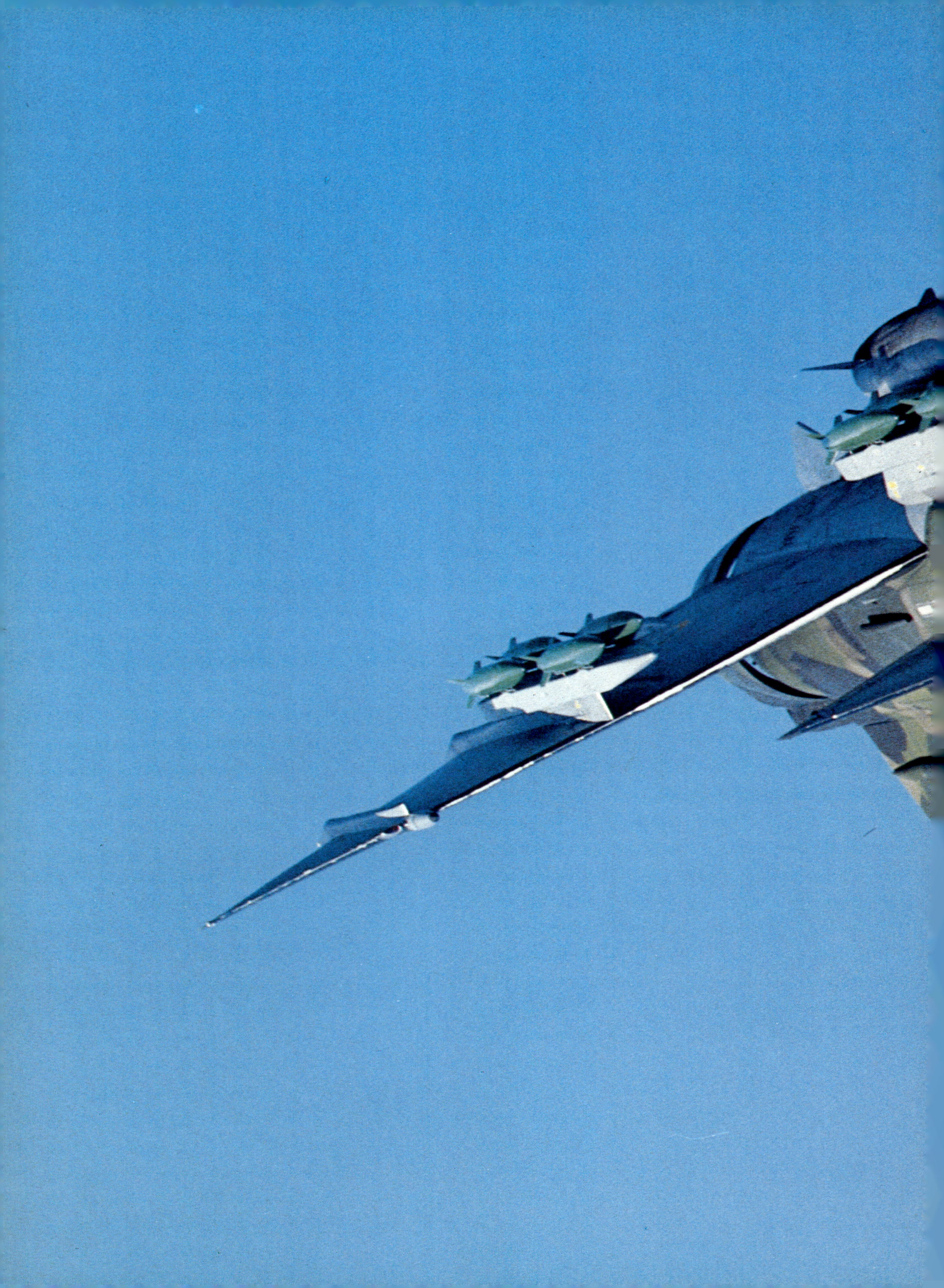

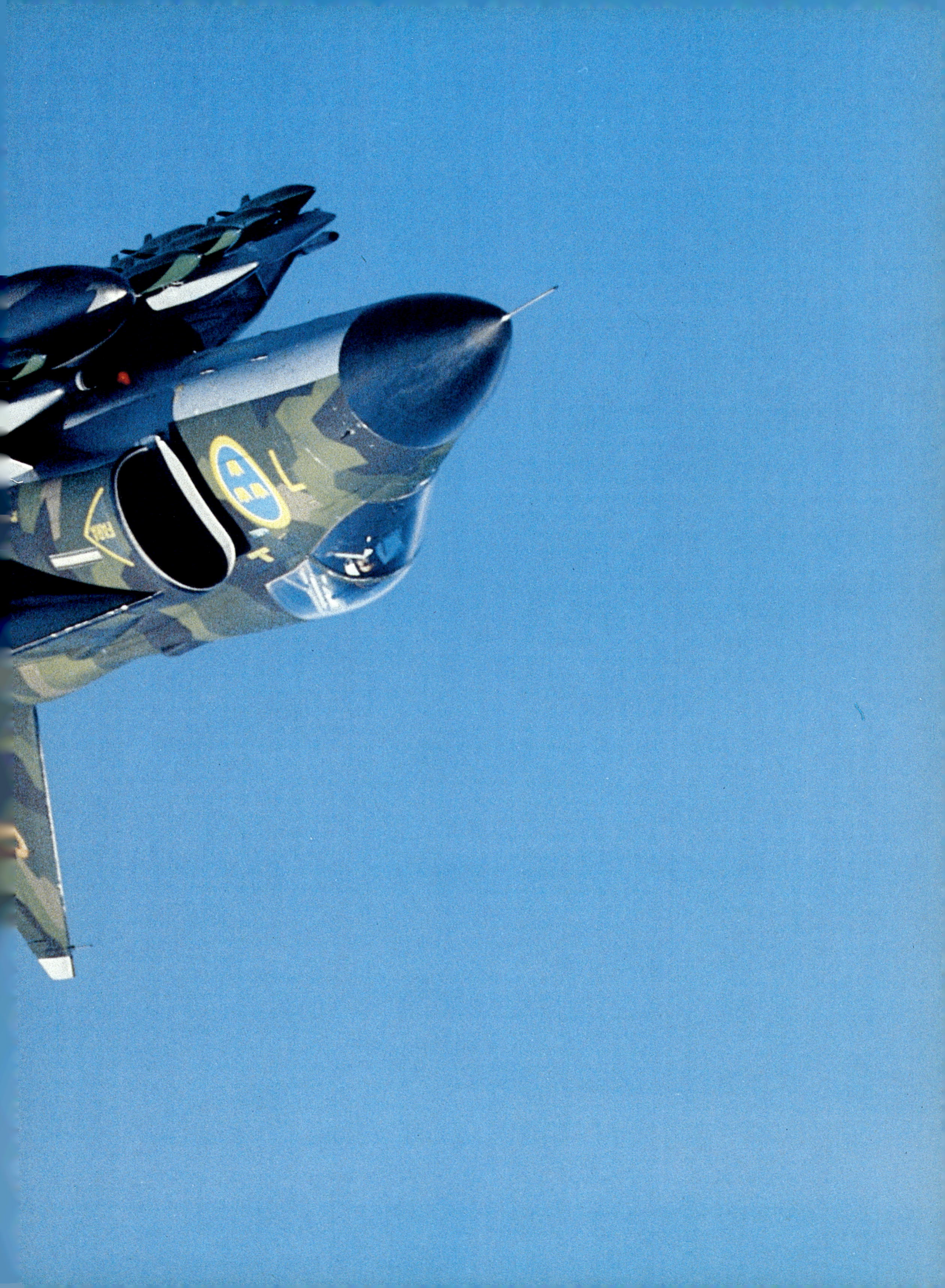

"Landing a fighter on a highway may sound easy, but I can assure you it is not. For us Swedish fighter pilots, it is part of our daily routine. Because of this, we will always be prepared for the possibility of our bases being wiped out by enemy bombers – the enemy could just as easily be a Warsaw Pact country as it could a member of NATO; everybody is just too close to our borders. Therefore, we put our money on mobile operations in Sweden. The location of most highway landing strips is common knowledge. Anyone who has driven through Sweden has seen the markings, but there are so many possibilities it will be next to impossible for the enemy to discover them all. Which we shall use is a secret daily decision.

"When it comes to normal runways, it sometimes just seems too easy for us. We can configure the plane in plenty of time and make our approach on instruments. Even masts and obstacles are clearly marked on our maps. On a runway, we have many more kilometers of concrete to land on than we can possibly use. With 8000 feet in front of you it is a piece of cake to get a Viggen into the air or on to the ground. But landing on a highway is *really* different. Obviously, we do not have the same types of instrument approaches available. You can, however, get a talkdown, a GCA (ground controlled approach) if there is a radar complex in the neigborhood. At 150 mph, the trees go mighty quickly past your head, and where there are trees there is turbulence. Because of this, as a rule, you put on some extra speed and you don't land with extra gas so you can reduce your final approach speed as much as possible and still maintain a comfortable margin above your stall speed. A highway strip is small in comparison to a runway, and you can't just go around like you normally would if your approach doesn't look quite right. You *will* put her down the first time. That certainty can make you a bit nervous.

"We also use frozen lakes. These, combined with our highway strips, allow us to operate independent of our bases from all over Sweden in time of war. A team of technicians can set up a highway landing strip in minutes. The pilot will then receive a heading from radar which will bring him to the newly set-up highway strip where he can refuel and reload. He also receives a low power frequency which carries about 20 miles. On this, ground control can direct him in for an overflight so he can orient himself with the strip and the wind direction. To be sure, he will make his first pass at 500' after which he'll turn aggressively to base and descend down to a 200' final. Normally, we begin our final turn at 1500', so it is a fairly steep final turn. The ground control will attempt to guide us in, but it happens much too fast. The pilot often makes his own approach. A Viggen can easily endure a carrier-like landing. That slam landing appears dramatic and it can be. You certainly leave a deep impression, but at least there's no doubt you're on the ground. You remain in the cockpit as the jet refuels and rearms. We can be airborne again in as little as 25 minutes, but under normal conditions we turn the jets around in 45 minutes to an hour. When the jet is gone, the base can be packed up and moved on to another spot, ready to do the whole thing over again. The way to perfect this form of operation is simple: you get to know your jet so well, that it's second nature to operate out on the extremes. That's how it is with my Viggen..."

Viggen pilot, Sweden

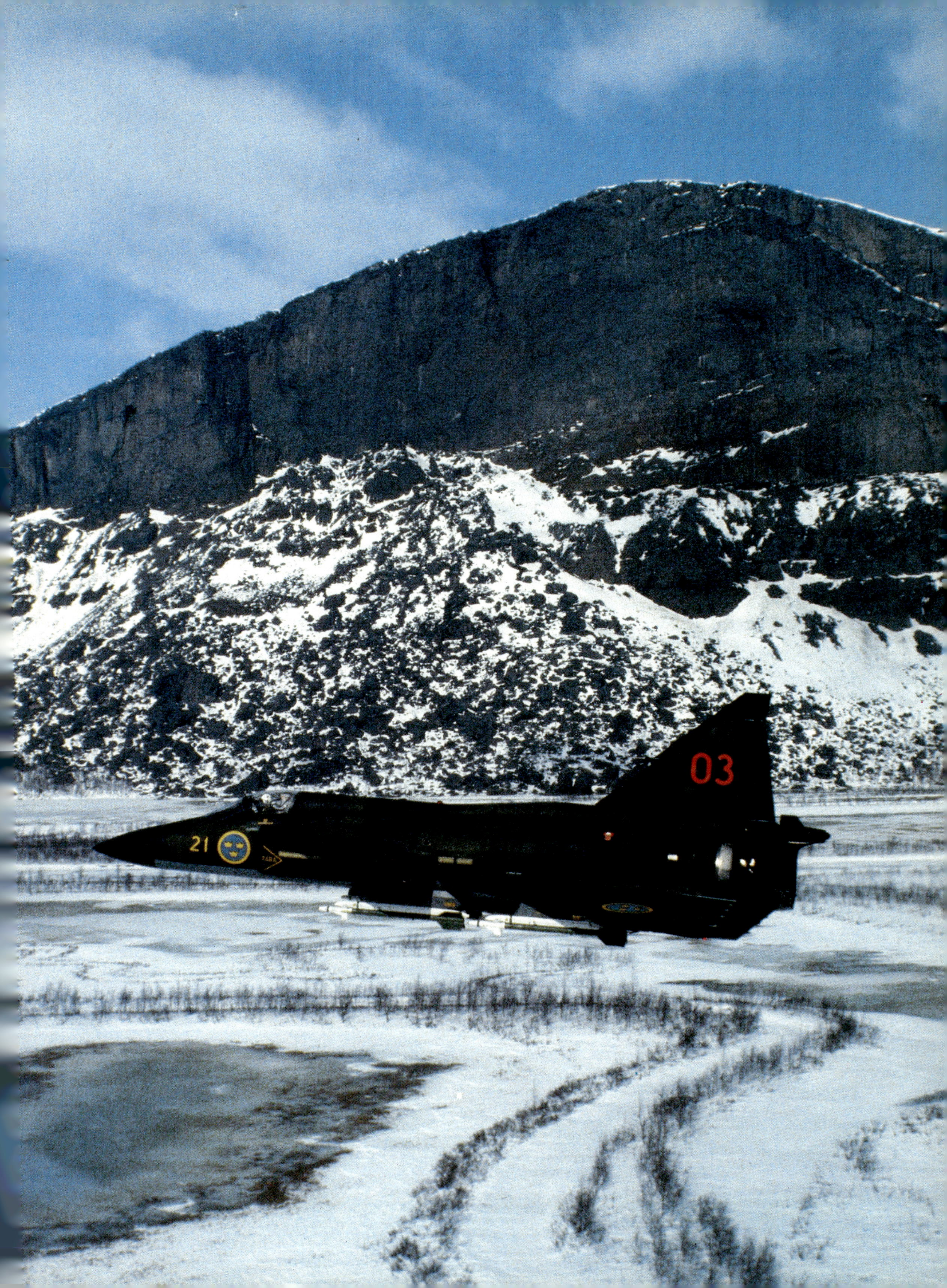
03
21

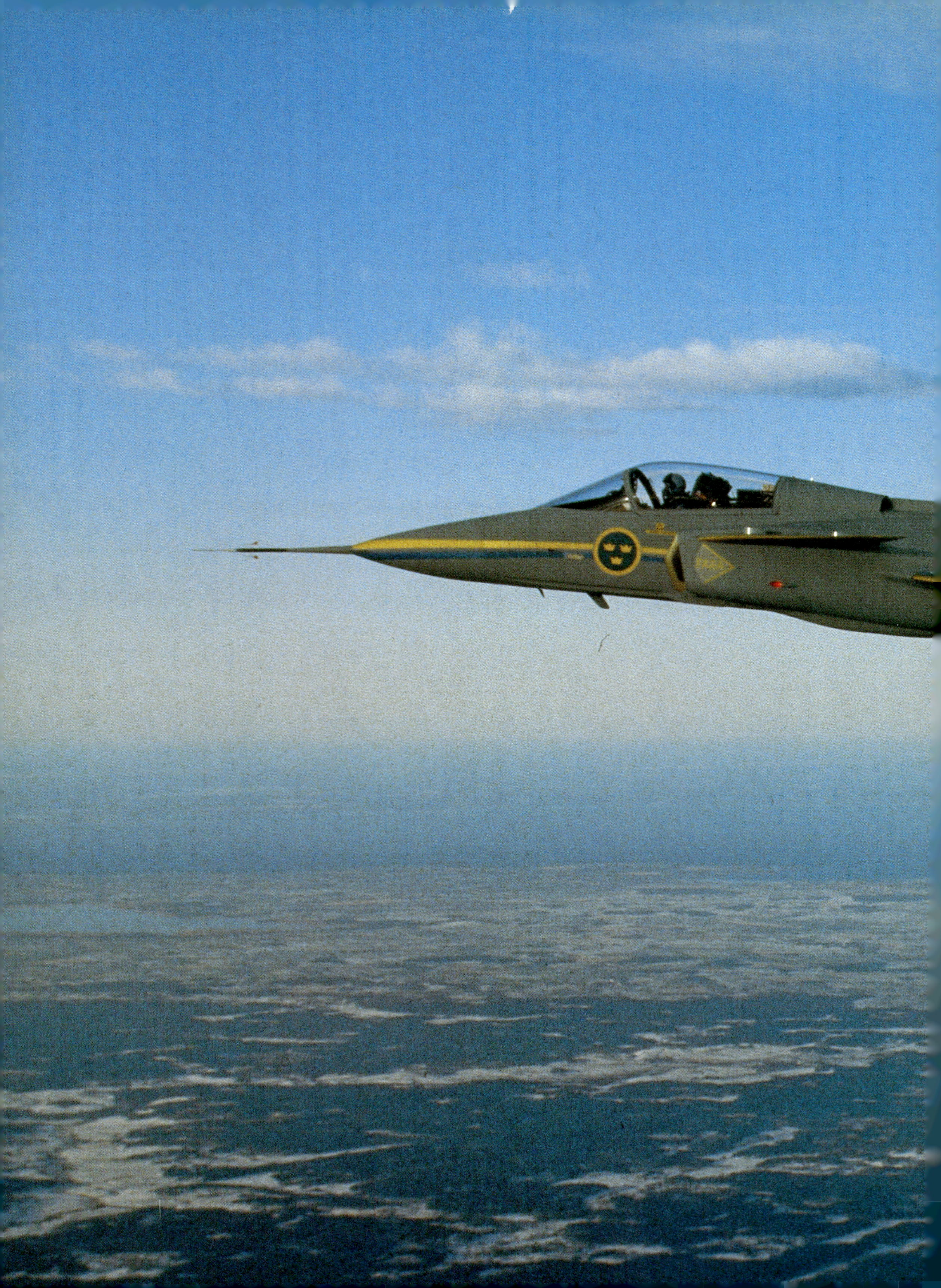

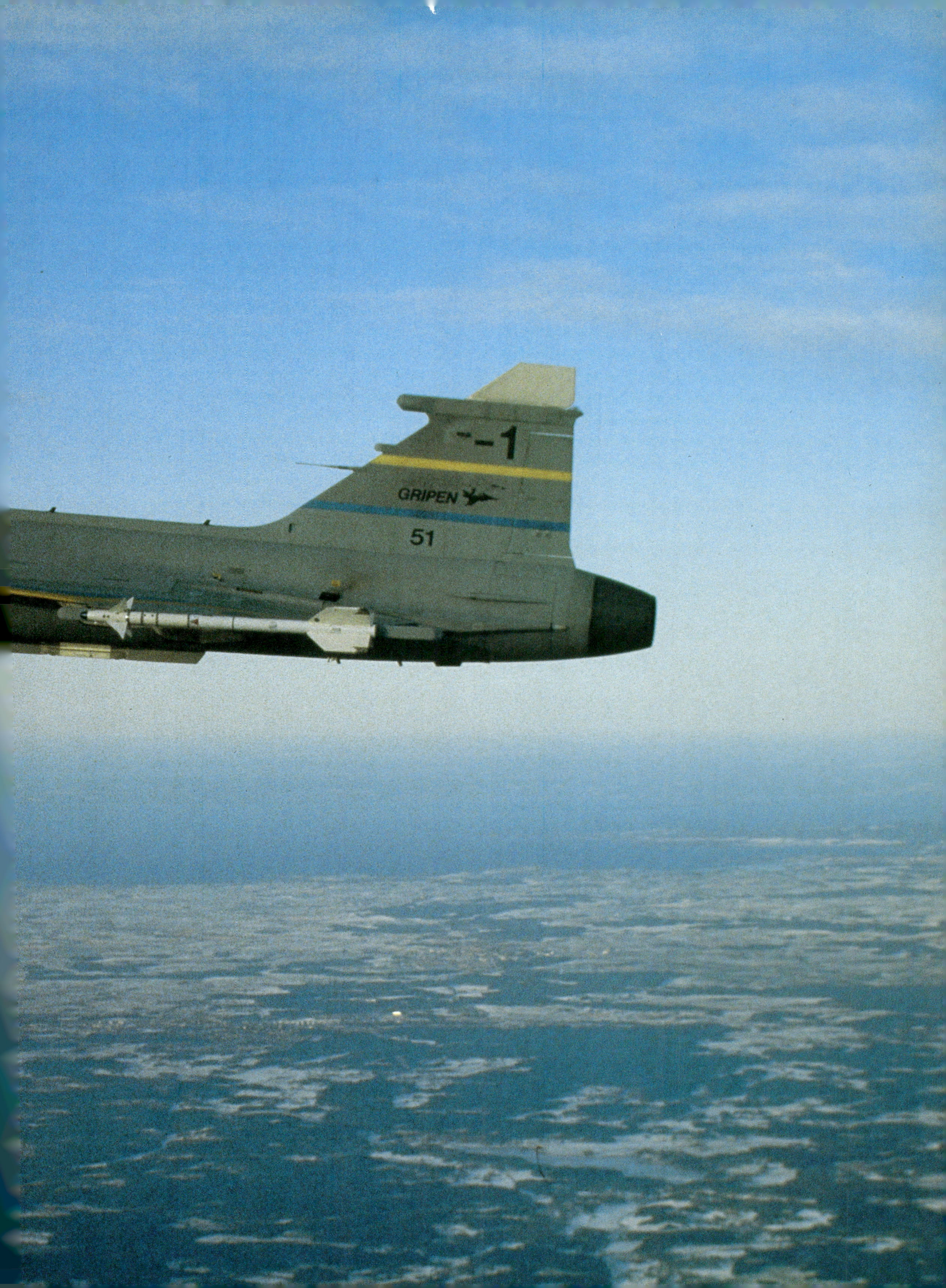
-1
GRIPEN
51

Sweden is a country with an amazing technological/ industrial complex. The Swedish people have repeatedly challenged it to produce the hardware which would allow it to maintain its position of neutrality in the world. Among those challenges, Sweden has asked for fighters which must be among the world's most advanced. The challenge has been met, time and again. The Draken was a remarkable achievement where the Swedes met their own demands with a radically different design. The result was a 1950's machine which is still viable today. The JAS 37 Viggen is an unbelievably effective fighter, the only one in the world which combines Mach 2 speed, fighter, bomber, and reconnaissance capabilities with minimum takeoff and landing distances. In fact, the Viggen almost appears to be making a carrier landing as it slams to the ground and stops surely on a fraction of the runway an ordinary fighter would have used.

The JAS 39 Gripen is Sweden's future in the air and if everything works out, it will be number one in the Swedish skies around the turn of the century.

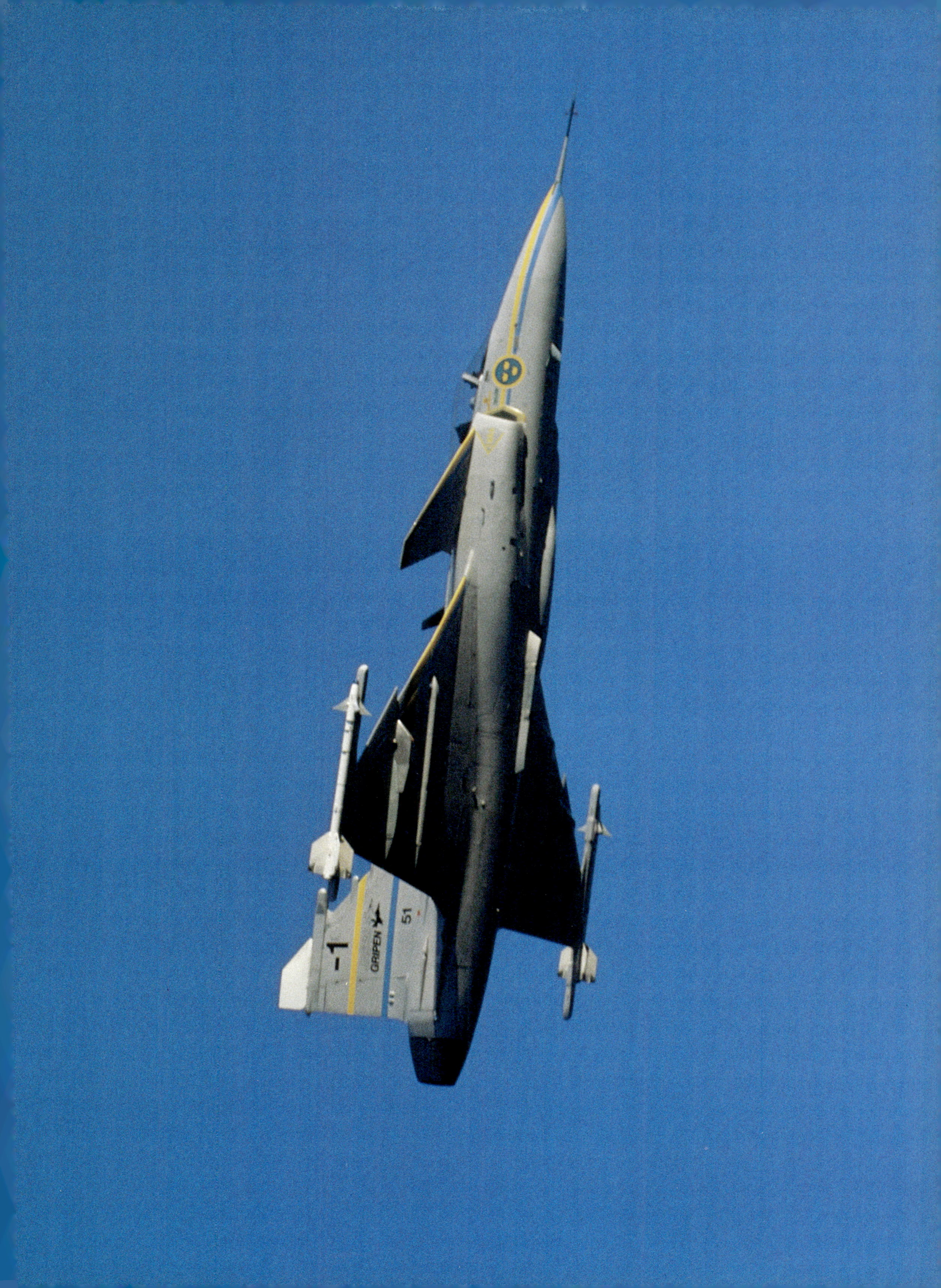
GRIPEN
51

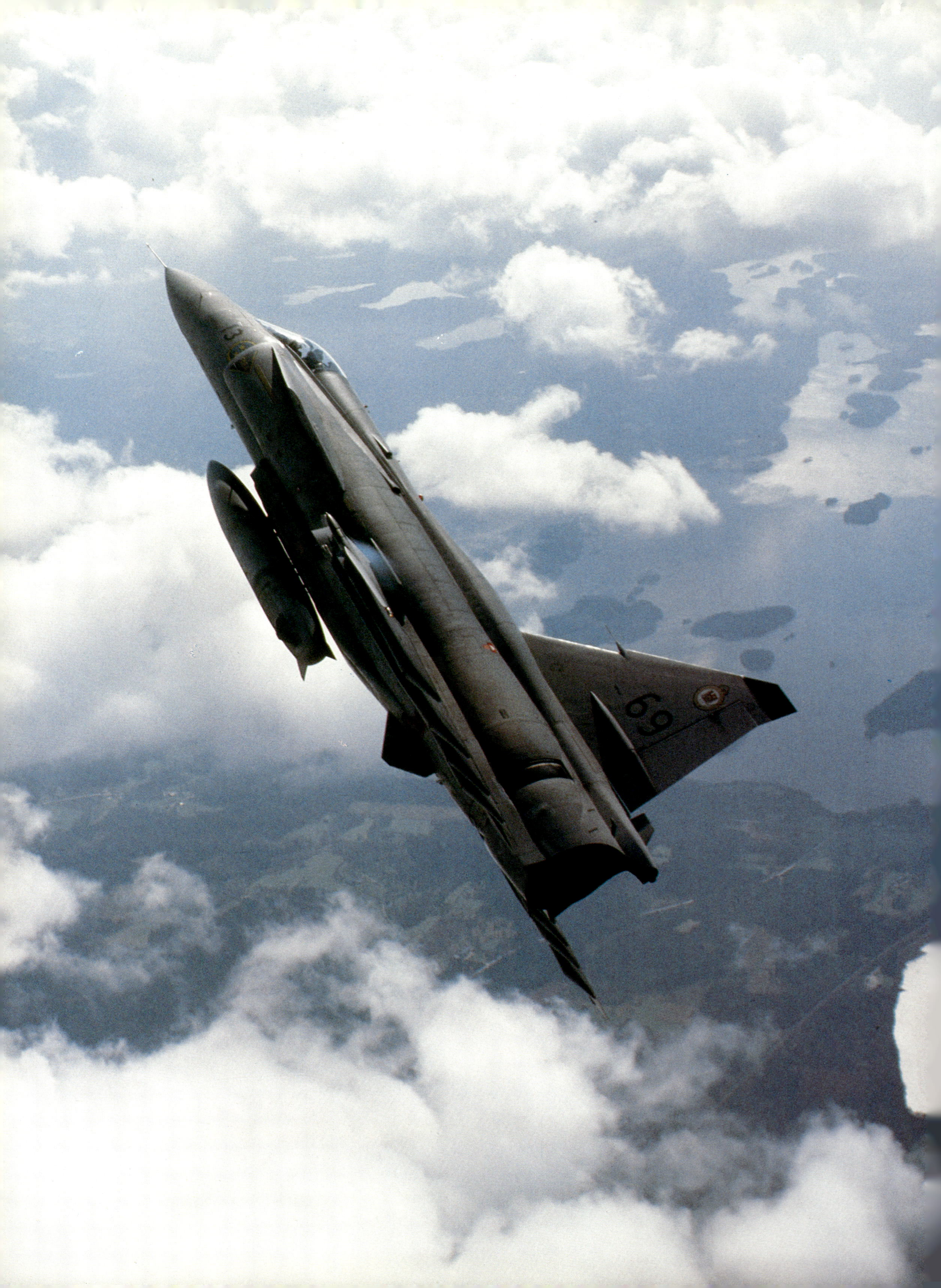
69

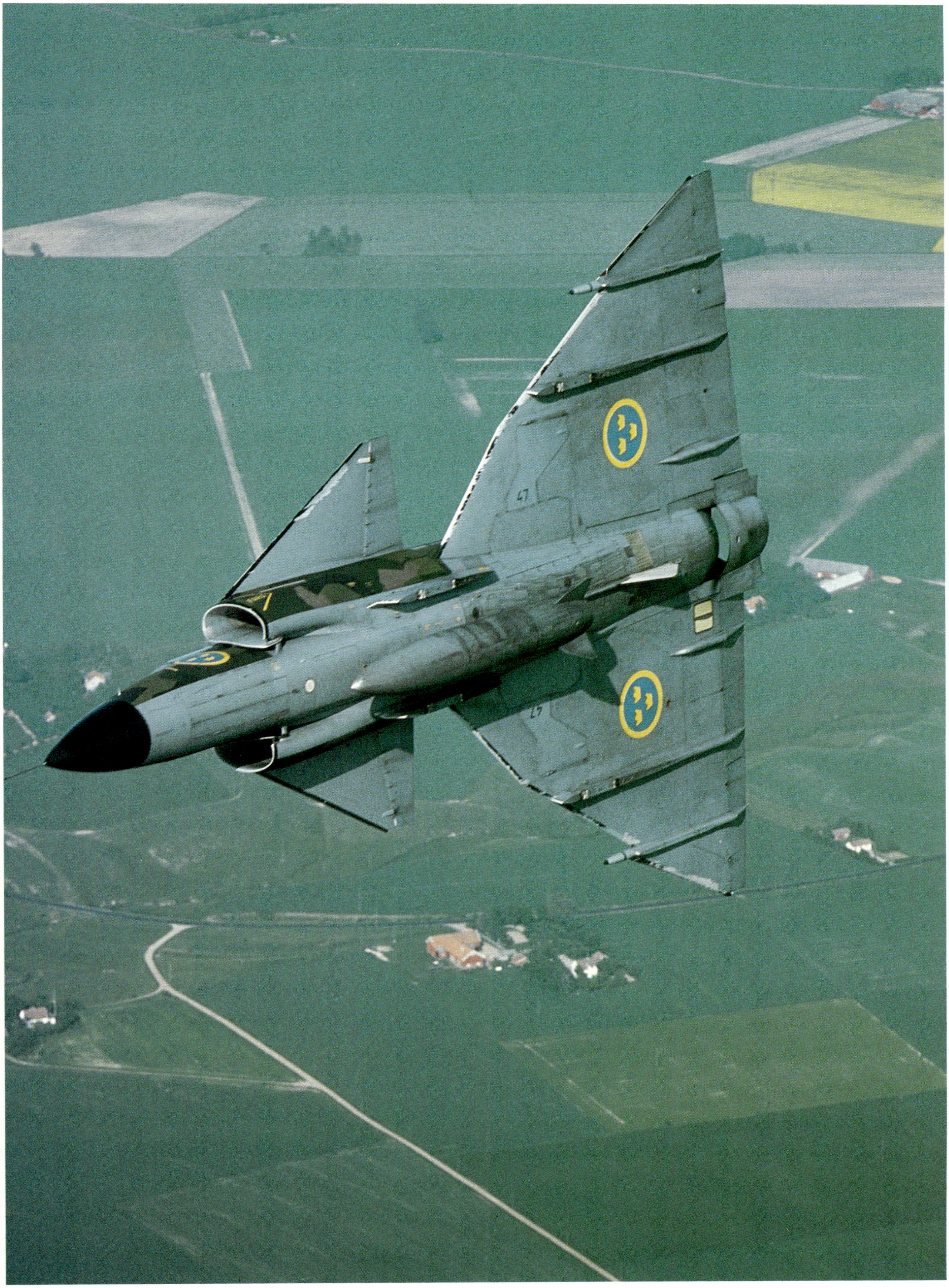

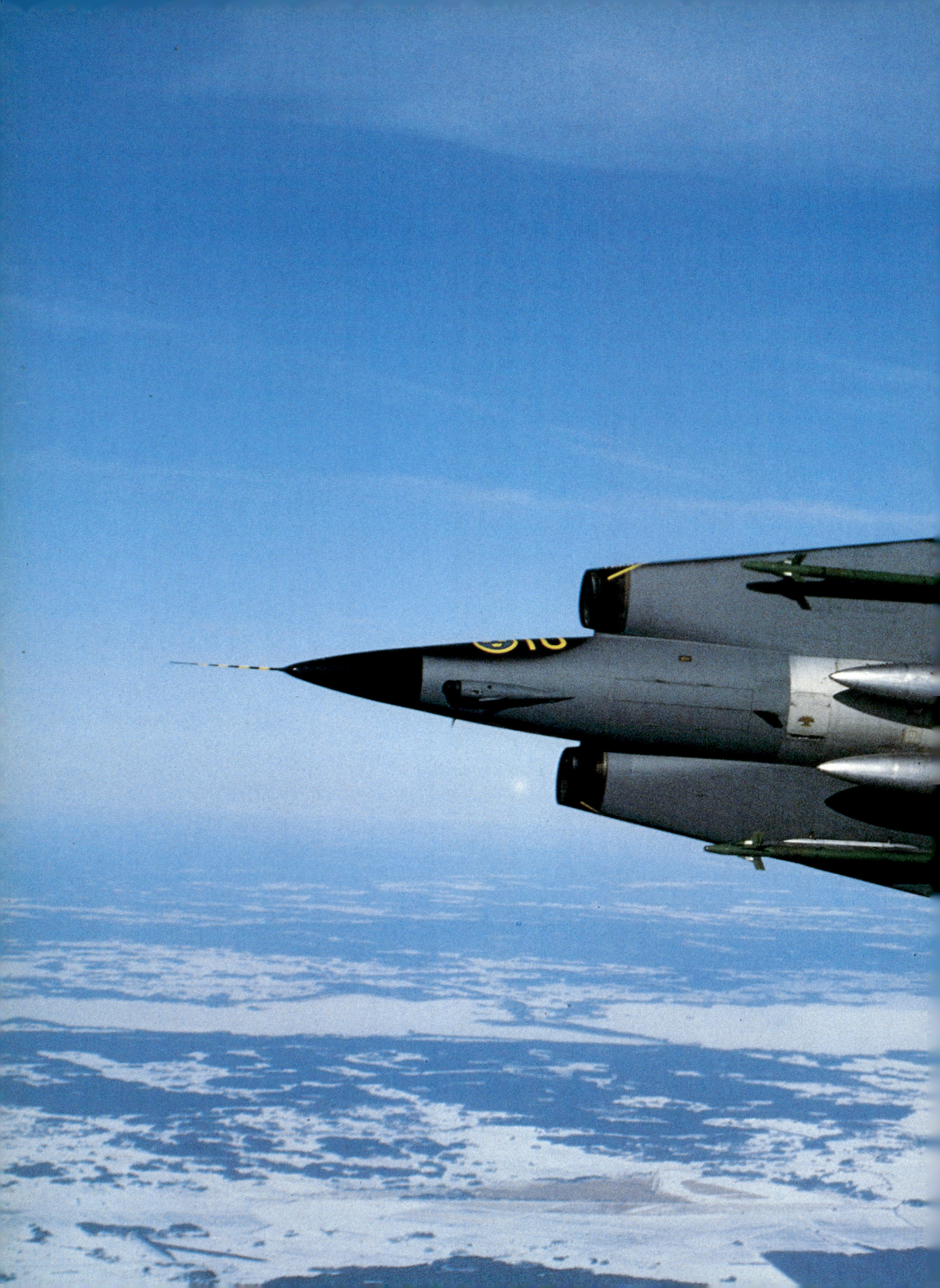

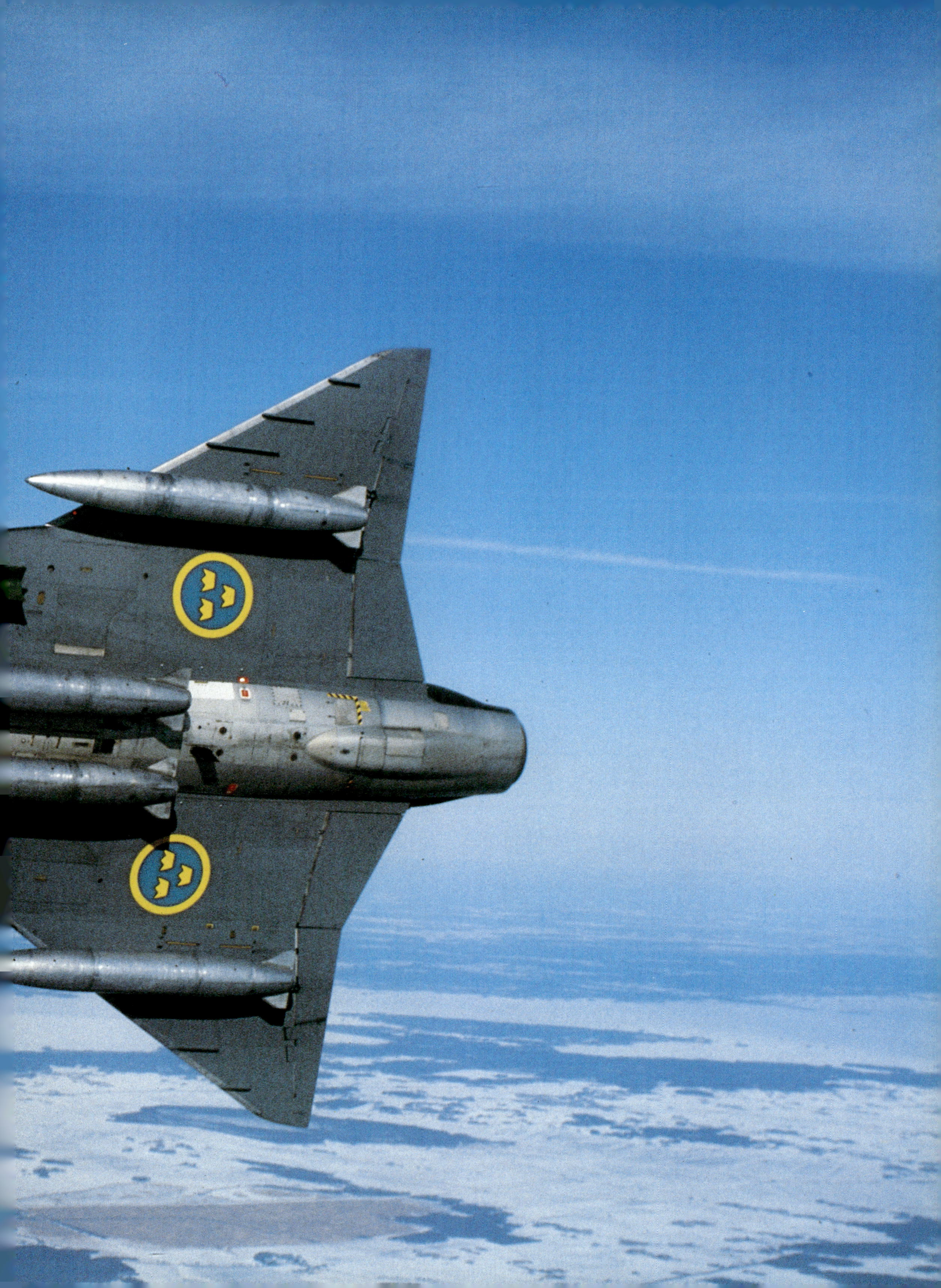

Sweden's Air Force is by far the largest in Scandinavia and among the largest in Western Europe. Although the Swedish Air Force has virtually the same number of employees as its neighbor, Denmark, Sweden operates approximately 500 fighters next to Denmark's 90. Because of their operational significance, Sweden fully expects all of its 16 major bases to be targeted in time of war. Nonetheless, radar and technical maintenance will continue out of the fortified, underground operations centers which are virtually impervious to conventional weapons. In keeping with this ideology, Sweden's best fighters, the Viggen, and shortly the Gripen, are designed to operate from highways, frozen lakes, fields, and beaches. The Viggen's STOL (short take-off and landing) characteristics are very similar to that of the British Harrier (see page 25), which can take off and land vertically. In the event of war, only NATO's Harriers and Swedish Viggens will operate independent from an airbase.

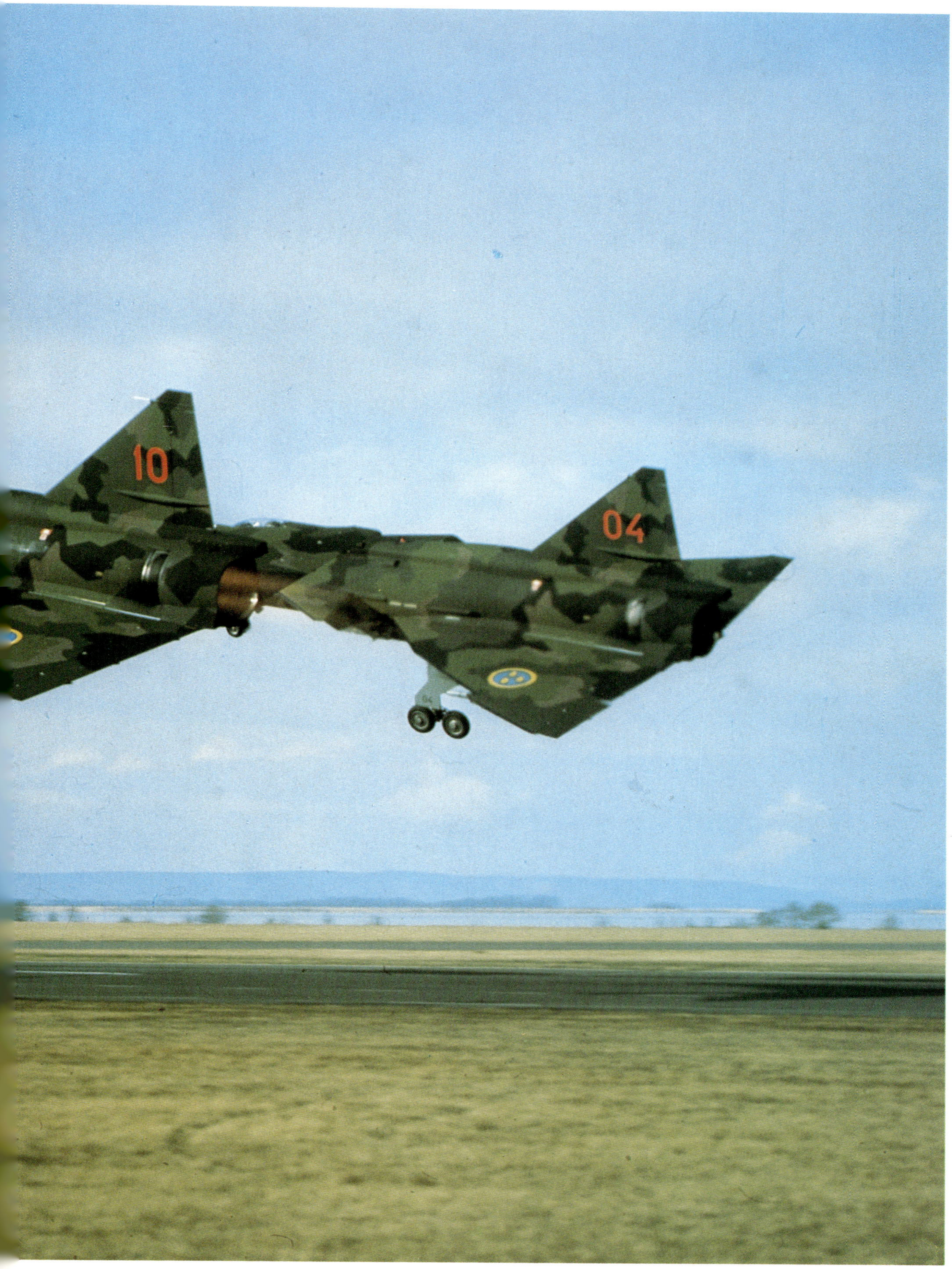
10
04

NORWAY

690

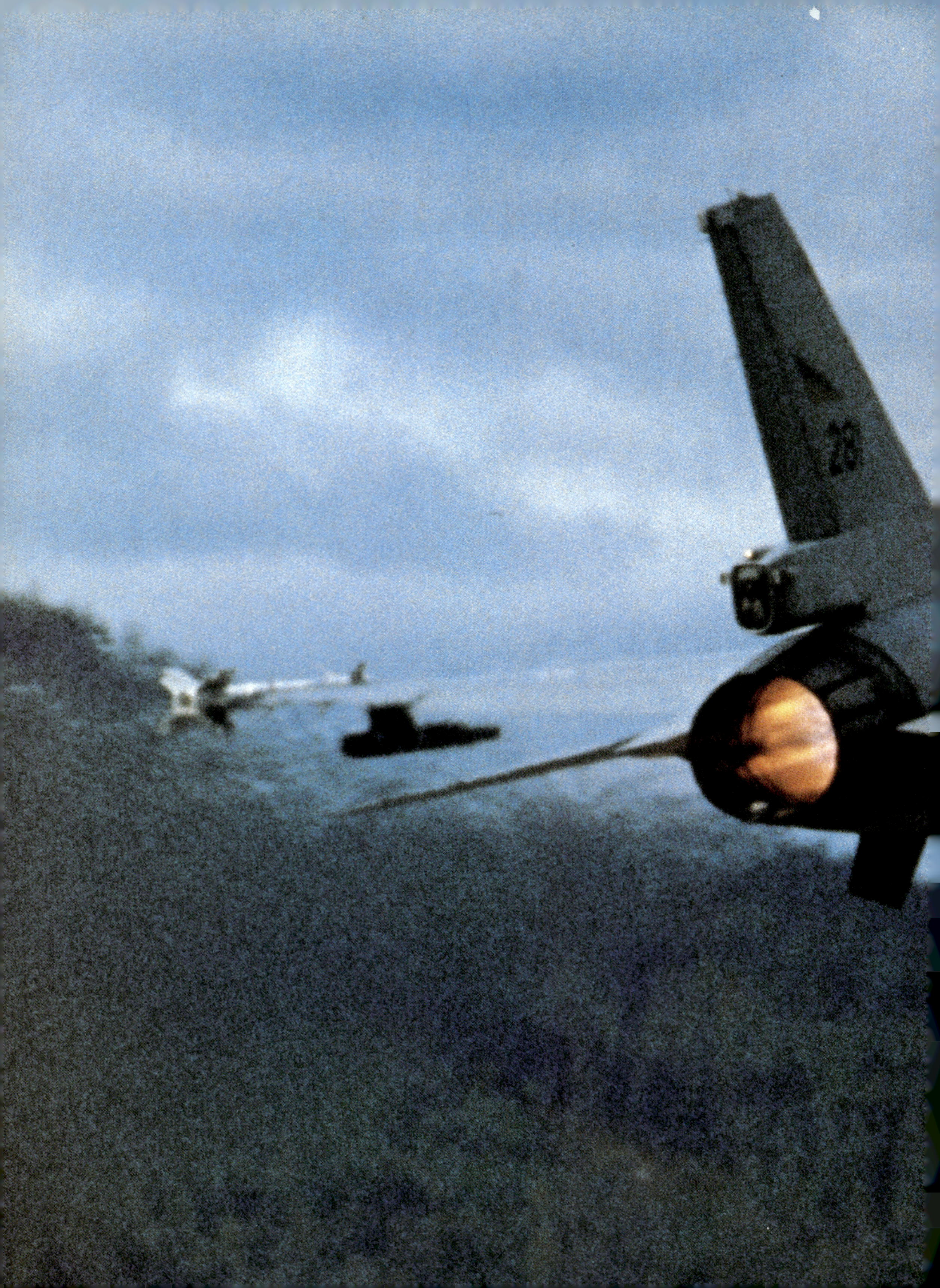
28

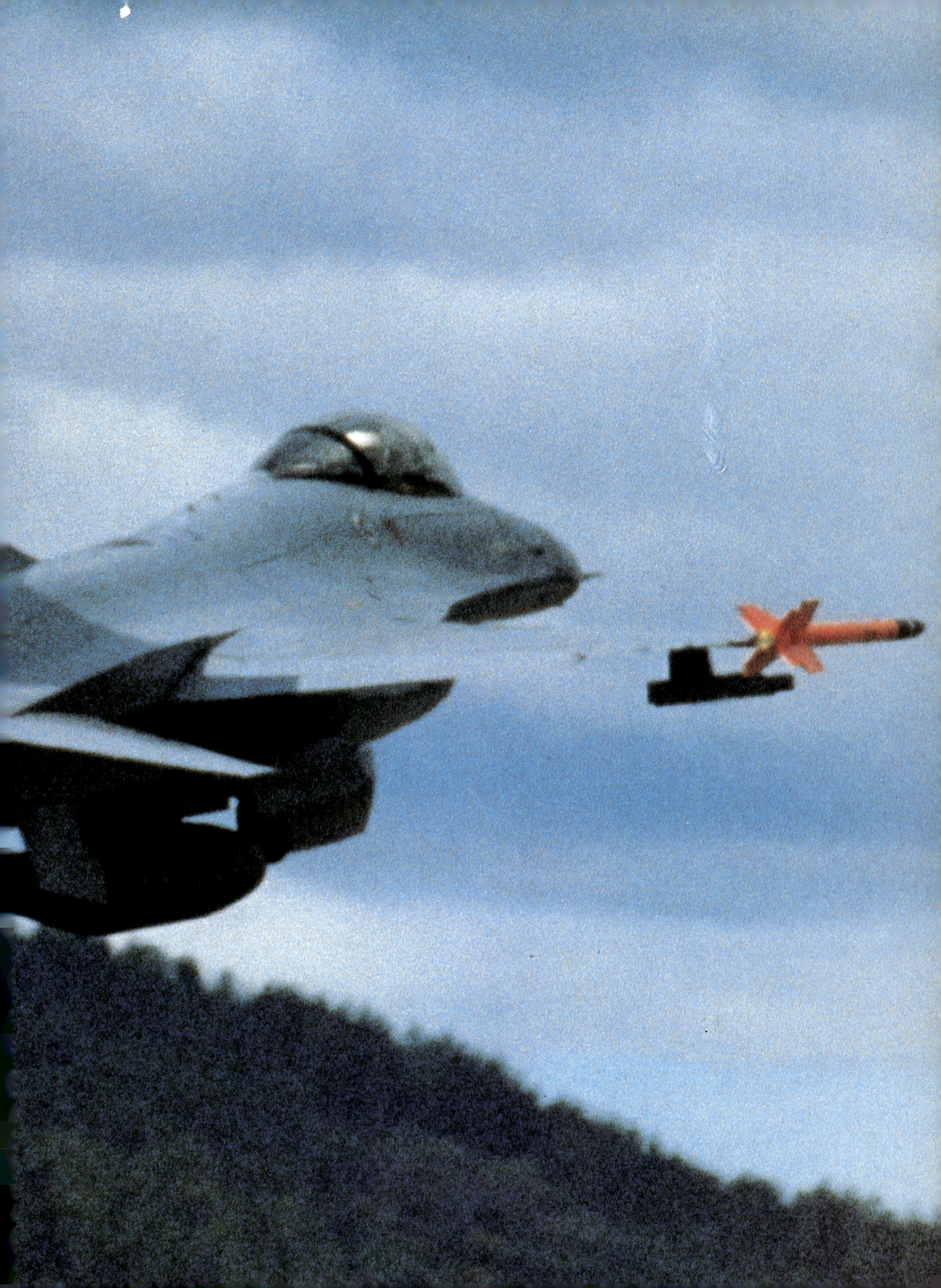

NADGE stands for a type of radar "Iron Curtain", a defense chain which stretches from Turkey to North Cape. While monitoring may be most intense in the so called "hot zone" around the actual Iron Curtain where both sides are constantly flexing their military muscles and the outbreak of aggression has always been feared, it is important not to forget the demanding task performed by the small nations on NATO's flanks. Among them is Norway, NATO's northern-most member – the land with the proud Viking traditions.

The landscape of Norway can be as harsh and unforgiving as it is beautiful and breathtaking. The terrain is so rugged that it is simply not possible to build the number of airbases which the country demands for its defense. Just building a runway long enough and straight enough for Norway's new F-16s has been made impossible by the surrounding environment. The Norwegian terrain appears to have been created for Vikings in bearskins and not pilots in flight suits. Norway's fjords provided countless natural harbours for the famous Viking ships with which the Vikings launched their expeditions to explore Iceland, Greenland, and America. These same fjords and rugged landscape make Norway next to impossible to invade. Perhaps it was the modern Norwegians' respect for mankind and desire to avoid a confrontation which allowed Nazi Germany to occupy the country so easily.

While Norway's geography has made it NATO's most unassailable country by land or by sea, it has also caused large problems in the day to day operations of an airbase. Norway's military aviation history goes all the way back to 1915, from which time the Norwegians have shed a lot of blood, sweat, and tears attempting to build a viable force in the skies over their homeland. The short, frozen runways in the treacherous northern Norwegian region demand a unique airplane, and because of this Norway is the only country using drag chutes on its F-16s.

The Royal Norwegian Air Force is one of NATO's smallest, but it is certainly effective. The pilots of the 65 F-16s and 30 F-5s, which comprise Norway's fighter Force, know their country inside out. To land in conditions seldom heard of in the USA is daily routine for them. Imagine fighting your way in through low ceilings and minimal visibility to a runway that is half as long as it should be. Add to that the fact it is covered with ice which requires not only perfect braking but the use of a drag chute to even stay on the runway.... pack all of these considerations into the minute you have on final approach while traveling at 150 knots and you'll realize today's Norwegian pilots are kindred spirits with their Viking ancestors who fought their way through wind and weather 1000 years ago.

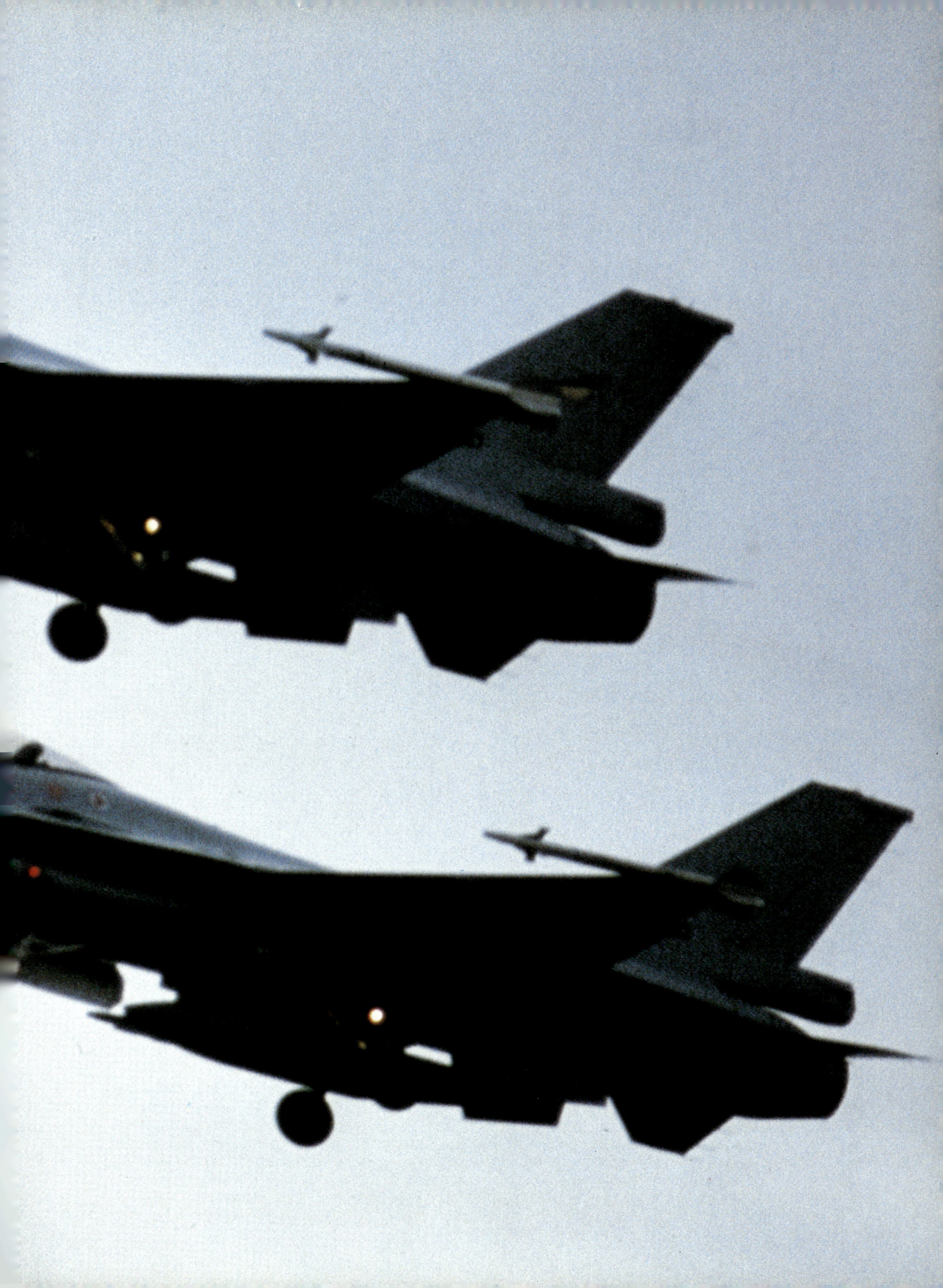

"When people hear that I am a fighter pilot, I never fail to get the classic response: 'Yeah, today it's so easy. In the old days the pilots didn't have all those fancy instruments. They were *real* fighter pilots.' They invariably conclude that it is the radar in the plane which makes our lives so easy because it allows us to find the enemy effectively and hunt him down. They always forget one thing: His radar allows him to do the same thing. In fact, he can even use our own radar against us.

"Let's take a typical intercept mission. I was sitting on alert one day when we were scrambled: Unknown aircraft inbound, course 270, altitude 3000 feet, speed Mach 0.8. Find him and destroy him if he is hostile.

"Six minutes later I slammed the throttle into full afterburner and I was on my way. I flew very low so I could come in under my target. Whatever it was, it would be easier to spot him looking up against a background of white clouds than looking down against the ground. The GCI (ground controlled intercept) controller, which we call 'Strike Control', gave me updated information about his course, but I didn't acknowledge over the radio. On this mission, we were observing radio silence because I didn't want to give myself away. I could have searched for him on my radar, but I had put it to stand-by. Modern fighters, on both sides, are equipped with sophisticated radar warning receivers which can detect radar waves. The strength and frequency of these waves can tell the receiver in which direction and how far away lies the threat.

"When GCI tells me I am roughly 30 miles from my target, I turn my radar on and acknowledge the radio call, for there is nothing left to be gained in the way of surprise. Now things start happening really fast. I light the burner and continue my intercept, trying to manoeuver in under and behind him. The tension really begins to mount. I am maybe 300 feet over the water doing about 550 knots – this gives a whole new meaning to the word 'speed'. I keep an eye on my altimeter and my fuel supply, because I'm burning gas at a tremendous rate with the afterburner on. At the same time, I'm trying to find him on my radar or, better still, pick him up visually. Now I have him. It is an F-16 just like mine. This isn't going to make things any easier. Luckily, I have managed to move in behind him and am able to hang on during his initial attempt to shake me.

(continued on next page)

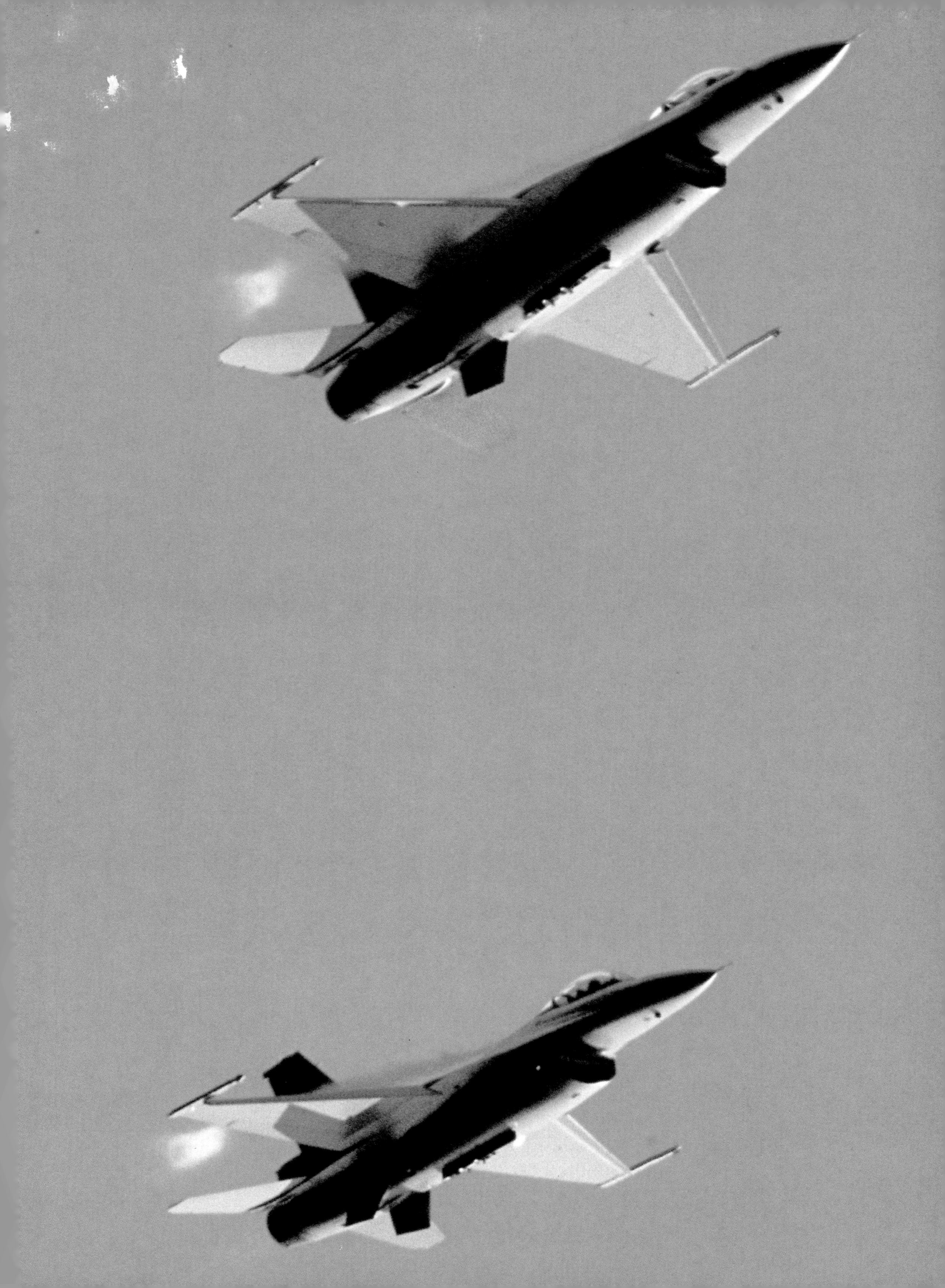

(continued)

"To hang on takes an 8 G turn – increasing my body weight 8 times more than normal. I remember my anti-G straining manoeuver which helps to stem the flow of blood from my head which occurs under high G. Unchecked, I would black out in seconds. My G-suit instantly inflates to help stop the pooling of blood in my legs. Fortunately, the HUD (head up display), contains all the information I need without having to take my eyes off my opponent.

"It is a very stressful situation – we have flown with electrocardiograms hooked up and it was not uncommon to find pulse rates in excess of 200 – but it is no easier for the enemy. We whirl around just over the water at breakneck speeds desperately trying to gain an advantage. I finally get him in my sights long enough to launch an air-to-air missile. The 'heater' streaks out from under my wing as I pitch up to avoid the fireball which would soon appear if I had actually launched an Aim-9. As my jet races upward, I roll quickly onto my side to see what's going on below. Instead of a fireball where my opponent used to be, I see the other F-16 racing away in another direction, aileron rolling as he goes. Pretty unfair considering I was the one who earned the victory roll!

Out of afterburner, up to 6000 feet, and back to the reasonable speed of 450 knots, I key the mike and calmly report 'target destroyed'. 15 minutes later I'm back on tower frequency getting my landing clearance. I see the runway in the distance and prepare for the challenging yet satisfying task of landing the F-16. The fight is long over, but under my flightsuit, oxygen mask, survival gear, and helmet the sweat

The border between Norway and the Kola peninsula, location of one of the largest Soviet military installations, has always been dangerous to get close to. Guided by the F-16's precise INS, these two Norwegian F-16 pilots carefully toe the line as they patrol for uninvited guests coming over into Norway.

Here, the F-16s escort a Russian Bear bomber back into international airspace. The Soviet Union has hundreds of these long range, turbo-prop bombers that, among other munitions, can carry atomic weapons.

Three generations of Norwegian fighters — two of which are still flying. The F-16 Fighting Falcon leads an F-104G Starfighter and an F-5 Freedom Fighter.

runs off me as I sit in the air-conditioned cockpit. The battle lasted just a few minutes, yet I realize the slighest error in this 'training engagement' could have meant death for either one of us.

"The last part of the mission is the debriefing. Here the 'enemy' and I review the flight: what happened, who screwed up, and why. We learn every time. Next time might be my turn to loose. The jet's video HUD film tells the tale of who was hit and why.

"There may have been many tremendous advancements in fighter technology, but no one will convince me it is easier than in the days of the Red Baron. Try the other way around."

F-16A Pilot

"You feel great the day you finally receive your wings at the end of pilot training. Now you can start to do some real flying. Now begins the real adventure.

"What was waiting for me in Norway makes the flying we did in pilot training seem like child's play. Norway is rugged country. The type of flying we do here doesn't resemble anything we did in the USA. In Texas, you could always look out the window of your T-38 (similar to the F-5 Freedom Fighter we still use in Norway) and see a piece of road or highway which looked suitable for use as an emergency landing strip. I never had to use one, but it was good to know it was there. In Norway you'd better refrain from looking outside too often if you want to enjoy your ride. All you can see are mountains separated by ice cold fjords, *if you can see* at all. Norway is notorious for its harsh weather. Weather which we didn't get a lot of training in coming from the USA. A shortcoming, however, which will be quickly solved. I can promise you that, because a Norwegian pilot does not become operational until he can land an airplane without seeing the runway.

"Harsh weather aside, I don't think you'll find a prettier land than Norway. To fly in the midnight sun over North Cape, at low level over the wilderness, or into the sunset over a fjord – I wish that many more had the opportunity to come and experience that..."

Norwegian F-16 Pilot

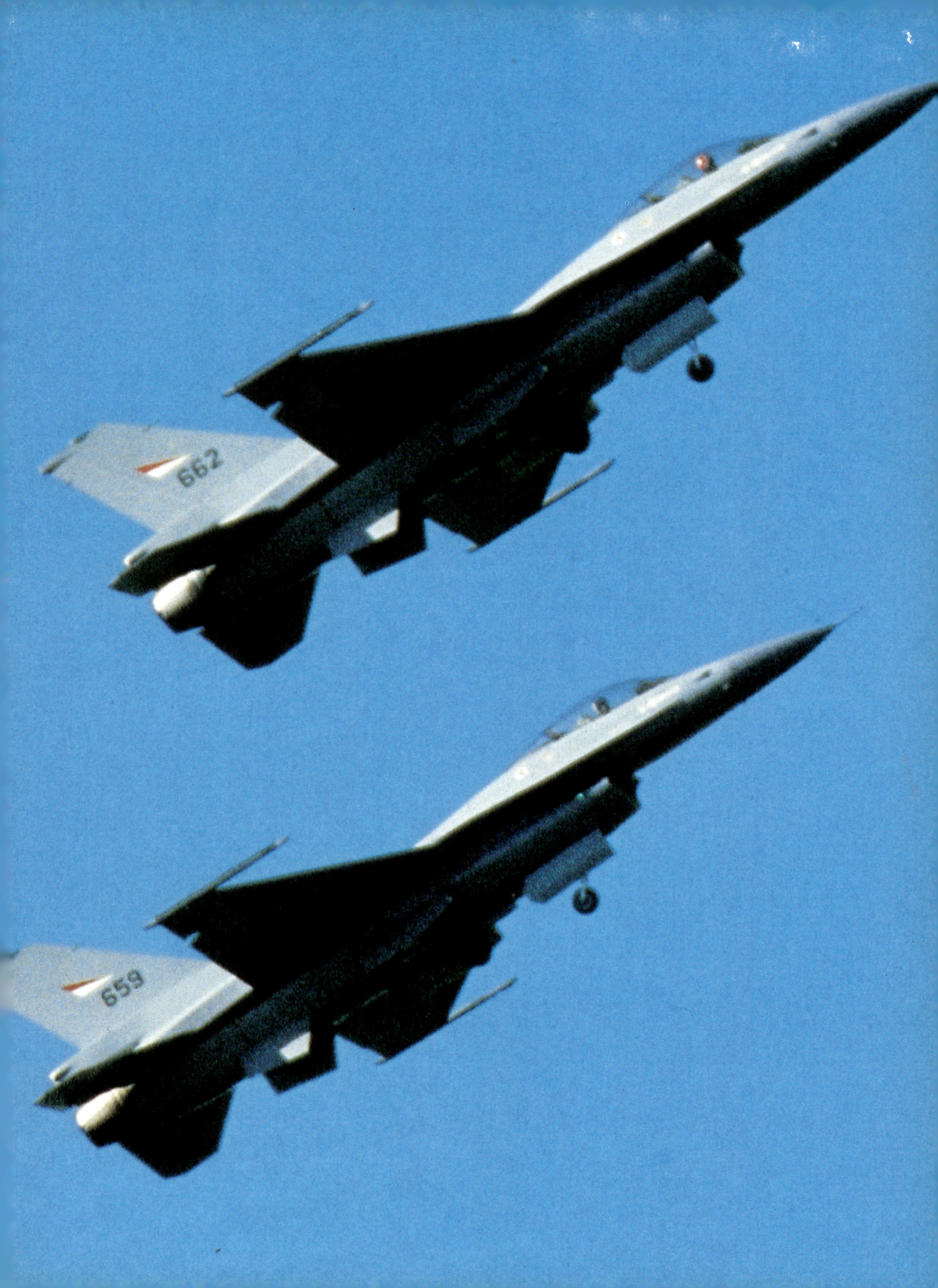
662
659

Today, NATO's premier fighter is the F-16, but for many years it was the F-104 Starfighter. No other fighter since has had a history as turbulent. Designed to be the US Air Force's premier fighter in the 1950s and able to fly faster and higher than all the others, Lockheed's "missile with a man in it" never received the Air Force's full support. There was something not quite right with this sleek and elegant fighter that from the start was infamous for its unforgiving nature. Nothing came easily behind the stick in the Starfighter, but if you were one of the few that could find the rhythm of that thundering beast you could make a formidable team. The US had trouble from the start finding a place for the F-104 in their system and as a partial solution began distributing them throughout Europe as part of foreign aid packages. The original Starfighter received a suite of additional avionics and became the F-104G. The airplane was now tremendously advanced, yet more dificult to fly as the additional weight of the avionics made the Starfighter's unique handling characteristics even more unforgiving. The reality of this surfaced differently from one European country to the next. For the pilots of Denmark and Norway, the F-104G proved a reliable fighter for 20 years. For the newly reformed Luftwaffe, however, the arrival of the Starfighter began one of the darkest chapters in German aviation history. West Germany lost a total of 118 F-104s: in 1967 alone, one every 10 days. Many crashes claimed the life of the pilot as few managed to eject. The reasons were many, but in general the combination of the Starfighter's unforgiving nature and the relative inexperience of the new Luftwaffe was simply destined to fail. As a result Starfighters were lost at an unbelievable rate and soon earned the ominous nickname "The Flying Coffin". A chilling example of the F-104's death toll took place over Northern Europe in the late 60s. Danish radar picked up an unidentified radar return crossing the West German border into Denmark. Two Danish Starfighters intercepted and identified a Luftwaffe Starfighter whose pilot was apparently unconscious. The Danish F-104s could do little more than follow the Luftwaffe Starfighter across Denmark and prepare for the unwanted task of shooting it down if it appeared that it might crash into a populated area. Over southern Norway two Norwegian Starfighters took over this agonizing mission. The Luftwaffe jet eventually ran out of fuel and crashed into the sea north of North Cape, the Norwegians following helplessly.

Many NATO countries flew the Starfighter, the Italians to the largest extent, and all would agree it was a formidable fighter in its day.

127